**Harvard
Business
Review**

on

SUCCEEDING
AS AN
ENTREPRENEUR

The *Harvard Business Review*
Paperback series

If you need the best practices and ideas for the business challenges you face—but don't have time to find them—*Harvard Business Review* **paperbacks** are for you. Each book is a collection of HBR's inspiring and useful perspectives on a given management topic, all in one place.

The titles include:

HBR on Advancing Your Career
HBR on Aligning Technology with Strategy
HBR on Building Better Teams
HBR on Collaborating Effectively
HBR on Communicating Effectively
HBR on Finding & Keeping the Best People
HBR on Fixing Health Care from Inside & Out
HBR on Greening Your Business Profitably
HBR on Increasing Customer Loyalty
HBR on Inspiring & Executing Innovation
HBR on Making Smart Decisions
HBR on Managing Supply Chains
HBR on Rebuilding Your Business Model
HBR on Reinventing Your Marketing
HBR on Succeeding as an Entrepreneur
HBR on Thriving in Emerging Markets
HBR on Winning Negotiations

Harvard Business Review

on

SUCCEEDING AS AN ENTREPRENEUR

Harvard Business Review Press

Boston, Massachusetts

Copyright 2011 Harvard Business School Publishing Corporation

All rights reserved

Printed in the United States of America

15 14 13 12 11   5 4 3 2 1

No part of this publication may be reproduced, stored in or introduced into a retrieval system, or transmitted, in any form, or by any means (electronic, mechanical, photocopying, recording, or otherwise), without the prior permission of the publisher. Requests for permission should be directed to permissions@hbsp.harvard.edu, or mailed to Permissions, Harvard Business School Publishing, 60 Harvard Way, Boston, Massachusetts 02163.

ISBN: 978-1-4221-7224-7

Library of Congress information forthcoming

Contents

Harvard Business Review

on

SUCCEEDING AS AN ENTREPRENEUR

Beating the Odds When You Launch a New Venture

by Clark G. Gilbert and Matthew J. Eyring

FOR NEARLY 20 YEARS the case study used to introduce Harvard Business School's Entrepreneurial Management course has been Howard Stevenson's "R&R." It looks at Bob Reiss, an entrepreneur who launches a venture in the board-game industry. Students are encouraged to explore all the production, development, distribution, and marketing costs associated with the new venture.

A cursory reading of the case suggests that it's a lesson in the rewards that come to an entrepreneur who is willing to take on an enormous amount of risk. Reiss capitalizes on what he correctly foresees is an ephemeral opportunity to ride the coattails of the Trivial Pursuit craze before me-too products flood the market. But a more careful analysis reveals something else entirely. At every turn, Reiss seeks to reduce his risks before making any significant financial investments or operational commitments. For example, he presells a sizable number of units to ensure cash flow. As students come to understand, Reiss actually limits his at-risk capital to the cost of the game design and the prototype. Rather than the high-risk, high-reward seeker he initially seems, Reiss proves to be a manager who constantly identifies risks and finds creative ways to remove them.

Over the past decade we have participated in the development of a dozen or so corporate ventures and served on new-venture boards at a host of companies, including Johnson & Johnson, the Scripps Media Center, and Landmark Media Enterprises. Although many of the ideas in this article come from our direct work with new ventures, they also reflect more than 10 years of collaborative thinking by the Entrepreneurial Management teaching group at HBS.

What has become clear to us is that the most effective corporate innovators are the ones who follow the same discipline Bob Reiss did. Success comes to those who quickly identify and systematically eliminate risks in the right order, using the right level of resources and the right methods.

Recognize That Not All Risks Are Created Equal

New ventures fairly bristle with risks. If managers attempted to eliminate all of them, the products or services would never get to market. The key question is "What's the most important uncertainty?" and the answer should be targeted early. In considering how to

Idea in Brief

Despite the popular image of entrepreneurs as risk-loving cowboys, the reality is that great entrepreneurs don't take risks—they manage them. The authors counsel managers to recognize that not all risks are created equal: When you're launching a new venture, first consider deal-killer risks that, if left unexamined, could kill the whole business. Next tackle the risks that could sabotage the project if it took a path you're not currently anticipating. Then focus on high-ROI risks—the questions you can answer without spending much money (but that will trip you up if left unanswered). Once you've identified the most important risks facing your new venture, manage those risks the way the best venture capitalists do: Spend a little bit of money at a time; create experiments that will test your assumptions; keep your timeline as short as you can; test only one thing at a time; and listen carefully for what an experiment's results are really telling you. Hint: You should be trying to prove that your assumptions are wrong, not simply to confirm your own biases.

answer that question, we have found it useful to think in three broad, sometimes overlapping categories: deal-killer risks, path-dependent risks, and easy-win, high-ROI risks.

Deal-Killer Risks

As the name implies, these are uncertainties that, if left unresolved, could undermine the entire venture. Such risks may be less obvious in the moment than they appear in hindsight, after catastrophe has struck. That's because they often take the form of unwarranted or unexamined assumptions about the premises underpinning the venture. For example, a colleague of ours was an early employee at a start-up satellite radio company aimed at consumers in the developing world. The premise of the venture was that satellite broadcasting technology would be a relatively cost-effective way to bring mass media to markets that lacked infrastructure. Market research suggested that a huge latent need would turn into a booming business. The company deftly negotiated broadcasting licenses in several developing countries and solved a number of complex technological challenges. Nevertheless, the business imploded. What was the problem?

As it turned out, the demand identified by market research depended on customers' being able to access the broadcasts through low-cost radio receivers—which turned out to be impossible. The radio receiver required complex features such as multimode playback, a keypad for ordering subscription services, and—worst of all—professional installation, which made the device unaffordable in most of the developing world. Having failed to identify this fatal vulnerability, the company invested hundreds of millions of dollars to reach consumers who couldn't pay for its service. The business limped along before ultimately going bankrupt. The company should not have left this key deal-killer assumption so utterly untested until late in the life of the venture. Quick-hit market research and rapid prototyping could have provided early warning signals.

Path-Dependent Risks
Rare is the new venture that never has to confront strategic forks in the road to success. Path-dependent risks arise when pursuing the wrong path would involve wasting large sums of money or time or both. For example,

consider the question confronting E Ink, a supplier of electronic paper display technologies in Cambridge, Massachusetts. In the company's early days there was great debate over whether its electronic "ink" would best be used for large-area display signage, flat-panel screens for e-books, or the more ambitious radio-paper products, which could be programmed and updated remotely. Each option had different technical, marketing, and distribution requirements; if the company chose wrong, it risked misallocating millions of dollars.

Rather than choosing one path and hoping for the best, E Ink reduced the cost of pursuing all three by outsourcing its marketing and production capabilities and then focused on resolving the risks associated with the core technology for all three applications. Thus, when display signage proved less successful, the company was not locked into a single market, and the technical knowledge it had developed allowed the fledgling venture to successfully license its technology for more viable products—most notably Amazon's Kindle.

Risks That Can Be Resolved Without Spending a Lot of Time and Money

Even after entrepreneurs have considered both deal-killer and path dependent risks, many uncertainties will remain on the table. If every one were addressed, they'd never get their products to market. But the more risks that can be eliminated, and the faster they can be removed, the greater the odds of success. Accordingly, successful entrepreneurs also look for risks that are quick and cheap to resolve, applying a cost-benefit approach that we think of as the "experimental ROI"—the amount of risk that can be reduced for each dollar invested in an experiment designed to resolve it. For example, one of the earliest experiments that Reed Hastings, the founder of Netflix, conducted in developing his movie-rental-by-mail business was to mail himself a CD in an envelope. By the time it arrived undamaged, he had spent 24 hours and the cost of postage to test one of the venture's key operational risks.

Fail to spot a deal-killer risk, and your venture is doomed. Fail to hedge a path-dependent risk, and you dramatically raise the odds that you'll run out of funds before you ever come to market—or will get there far too late. Fail to address a high-ROI risk in an orderly way, and you may transform a temporary setback into an insurmountable obstacle.

Such was the fate of a start-up we worked with that targeted the nascent medical tourism market. The venture's value proposition was to fly patients overseas for high-quality, inexpensive medical care, which it expected to deliver at half the cost of the same care in the United States. Several deal-killer risks faced the venture. Unfortunately, rather than tackling them early, by beginning with those that could be tested most quickly and at the least cost, team members plunged into a time-consuming and expensive effort. To gauge demand, they conducted a series of long interviews with *Fortune* 500 corporate benefits managers and insurers around the country. Things looked very promising. However, not until they'd put in nearly six months of work and spent considerable money on travel did they decide to do something they should have done early on: run two simple, high-ROI experiments to test key risks. The first involved a seminar to introduce the concept to prospective patients. The second involved several phone calls to U.S. hospitals to discover their unpublished discount prices for certain procedures. In only two weeks (and at virtually no expense), the team learned that patient demand was actually quite tepid and limited to a very narrow band of procedures, and that U.S. hospitals were willing to lower their prices—to near international levels in some cases—if patients paid cash up front. By failing to address their greatest risk—that no market existed for their services—in the cheapest and fastest way, the team members wasted significant resources and missed a critical opportunity to redirect their strategy to something more promising, such as a venture restricted to regional medical travel within the U.S or travel to a close international destination like Mexico.

A common mistake is to focus on one key risk to the exclusion of others. Sometimes you must be satisfied with partial risk resolution in one area, even as you start to consider and work on risk in another. As a general rule, we have found it's best to select a "stake in the ground" customer early in the life of the venture. You can then confirm a rough price point at which customers can be served, even as you continue to reduce related technical risk.

Tackling the Right Risks First

RISK AND VALUE ARE INVERSELY PROPORTIONAL: When you remove risk, you increase value. But it matters in what sequence you tackle risks, because not all of them are created equal.

Suppose a manager is launching a new e-commerce business. He must remove a number of risks before the venture reaches its peak value. He could simply remove them as they occur to him.

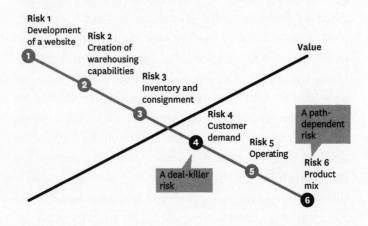

Be Judicious with Capital

All other things being equal, a large corporation's deep pockets should give it an advantage over bootstrap entrepreneurs when it comes to financing a new venture. But in practice, a parent company's funding procedures are often a major liability—something one of our colleagues, Brad Gambill, has referred to as "the curse of too much capital." Corporations typically allocate money for a new venture all at once, hoping for a large payoff fairly soon. The more money that is sunk into a

But unless he confirms demand, it doesn't matter how provocative his website is; customers won't buy. And if he doesn't answer the product-mix question, he will fill his warehouse with products he can't sell.

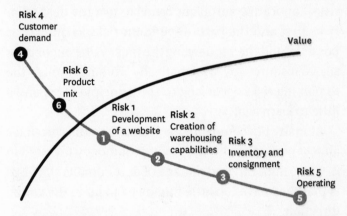

Addressing these two risks early creates disproportionate value quickly, not only saving critical resources but also moving the venture in the right direction sooner.

project at the outset, the less patience the company tends to have and the more people believe in the validity of their original approach, even in the face of evidence to the contrary.

The way venture capitalists invest in start-ups—by providing capital in multiple rounds as the value of the venture increases—is far more effective. As one of our colleagues puts it, "With each risk you pull off the table, value goes up proportionally." The lower the risk, the greater the value, so this approach favors entrepreneurs who use early funding to reduce the greatest

When Risks Are Overlooked . . .

FEWER THAN 15% OF FIRMS are still in operation three years after initial funding, according to one study of venture-backed start-ups.

risks—allocating sufficient funds to test the deal-killer risks first and the path-dependent risks as quickly as possible, and then squeezing the most value out of their scarce resources by systematically working through the remaining risks according to the principle of "spend a little to learn a lot."

At many big companies, a project's status correlates almost perfectly with the amount of money invested in it. The competitive advantage of autonomous start-ups is that they have too little money to go far in the wrong direction.

We can demonstrate the power of this dynamic with two very different examples. Vermeer Technologies, a start-up based in Cambridge, Massachusetts, had only one product: a website development tool called Front-Page. The company was eventually sold to Microsoft, and Microsoft FrontPage became the most widely used web-design software package in the world. But that's not where Vermeer's strategy began. In the early 1990s its founders had hoped to create an interface that would allow users to access content through a common reader across a wide network of computers all over the world. There was only one problem: A nascent service—the World Wide Web—was free to anyone who wanted to access it. After Vermeer's founders learned more about the Web, they decided to take another path altogether, devising a software tool that let nontechnical programmers create their own websites. Reflecting on their original strategy, the founders laugh in relief that they didn't make any significant investment at the outset, because they might have poured their capital into building an ultimately worthless company.

An equally instructive example with a less fortunate outcome is that of Joint Juice, a Bay Area company founded by an orthopedic surgeon who came up with the breakthrough idea of converting glucosamine, effective in reducing joint pain, from a large pill into a more convenient liquid. A strong conviction that his target market was young to middle-aged athletes led to a series of expensive choices relating to the product's caloric load, packaging, distribution channel, and marketing approach. Lavish advertising campaigns were built around professional and Olympic athletes. These early, high-cost investments became self-reinforcing.

Just as data were beginning to reveal that the real demand lay with an older demographic—people who wanted lower-calorie, less-expensive products—an opportunity arose to go national with two large grocery chains. Sunk costs made the opportunity more tempting than it should have been, and Joint Juice signed an expansion contract replete with the high slotting fees associated with grocery retail. When it became clear that the channel and market were wrong, the enterprise was already locked in to a product incorrectly formulated, positioned, and distributed. Today Joint Juice has been adapted to the right market, but only after millions of dollars more were invested—and significant changes were made to the management team.

We cannot make this point too strongly: At the start of a new venture, the only thing you can know about your initial strategy is that it's probably part right and part wrong. One of our colleagues conducted a study of the *Inc.* 500 entrepreneurs and found that most successful ventures had redirected their strategy at least five times before they hit a solid growth trajectory. If you go full speed in your first direction, you'll compromise your ability to figure out which part is wrong—and pay a high price when you eventually do figure it out. But if you invest in stages, spending small sums on the assumption that your strategy will need adjustment, you'll find it much easier to adapt quickly and reach a winning outcome.

Manage Experiments Efficiently

Identifying and prioritizing risks correctly and then conceiving and funding experiments to resolve them systematically will make the unpredictable process of launching a new venture as efficient as it can be. You can take several steps to make your experiments more effective.

Limit the Duration
According to Meg Whitman, the former president and CEO of eBay, the company succeeded in its earliest days by recognizing that perfection is sometimes the enemy of the good. It's often better to get something into the market quickly, learn from it, and move on to the next phase of development than to analyze an idea to death

and try to perfect it before launch. Even deal-killer risks can sometimes be tested quickly and simply. For example, Innosight Ventures saw an opportunity to serve consumers in India who couldn't afford washing machines but wanted an alternative to the traditional *dhobi* services, which are slow, use dirty water and inferior detergents, and beat clothes on rocks to remove the water from them. The venture managers needed only 60 days to move from completion of the business plan to an initial market test. The test was simple but powerful: They invested a few thousand dollars to build a kiosk that contained a washing machine and a dryer and put it on a busy street corner to see if people were willing to pay 40 rupees (about $1) per kilogram to wash their clothes. It was essentially a mini-launch designed to answer the key question in their business plan: Is there unmet demand for an inexpensive laundry service? Several weeks of growing customer demand at the site indicated a high likelihood that the concept and pricing were essentially sound and with further refinement could exceed estimated break-even levels. Today more than two dozen kiosks have been set up in several Indian cities, and there are plans to expand the business to more than a thousand over the next few years.

Test One Thing at a Time

Poorly designed experiments vary too many factors at once, increasing the expense and making it difficult to determine what causes what. Experiments should be simple and focused on resolving uncertainties one by one. At a large media company we worked with, the

Test Early, Test Cheaply

PERHAPS THE MOST DANGEROUS RESULT of injecting too much money too soon into a venture is that it creates a confirmation bias in the minds of venture managers. Instead of testing their assumptions, they become more and more invested in confirming them. But successful entrepreneurs do the opposite: They devise low-cost experiments to disprove a concept before it's too late.

We've found two types of experiments helpful in our work.

Targeted Experiments

These are designed to pinpoint a deal-killer or path-dependent risk. Examples might include running tests on battery life before launching a new portable device, checking for toxicity in a drug before running full-scale efficacy tests, and testing bandwidth and connectivity concerns before launching an online learning program at various locations across the country.

Integrated Experiments

These are designed to test how various elements—the actual business model and operations—work together. In essence, they

---

venture managers ran experiments to test a new website registration system that would allow them to target various demographic segments with ads. They didn't know whether registration should be required or optional. Accordingly, their experiment was designed to answer the questions Will people be discouraged from visiting the sites if they are forced to register? and Will people register at all if they aren't required to? Instead of running tests over an entire network of websites, they picked two comparable sites and for a month ran one with an opt-in registration and the other with a involve launching the business, or some part of it, in miniature. Although pilot programs are nothing new, our experience suggests that entrepreneurs rarely give them sufficient time to play out. An exception is Aaron Kennedy, who founded Noodles & Company, a chain of quick-casual restaurants. From the beginning Kennedy intended to take his concept nationwide, but he started with just three restaurants. He revised the menu, varied the décor, and tested several pricing structures. For almost an entire year he focused on sharpening the concept and making it work on a small scale. Today the chain has more than 218 locations in 18 states.

An integrated experiment may be a pilot, a test-site location, a prototype, or any other trial operation. It might include tests to "launch" the business in a way that allows customers to purchase the product in a real transactional environment. Targeted experiments such as surveys and focus groups can provide insights, but those that come from placing the product in a sales channel where customers make actual purchase decisions are often much deeper.

forced registration. Everything else was held constant—promotion, launch, investment, and so forth. When the forced registration didn't reduce site visits significantly, they had their answer.

Apply the Lessons Learned

Too often managers miss the whole point of these experiments. They are meant to help redirect a venture, not to confirm that your initial ideas were correct. Some of our colleagues call this discovery-driven learning. Recall the data on the *Inc.* 500 ventures—five major course corrections for every successful venture. Sometimes those corrections come painfully, but it's better to choose to adjust early than be forced to adjust later.

Be Willing to Turn Off Experiments

This idea is closely related to the previous point, but requires far more discipline. Some ventures are simply not going to work. A deal-killer risk may in fact kill the deal. The sooner you cut your losses in such cases, the sooner you can go on to the next venture. More often, though, the principle applies to some specific component of the venture. We've watched executives in the newspaper industry struggle with this as they've tried to migrate from print media to digital content. One senior manager confessed to us, "We had a thousand experiments running; some of them were working and some of them were not. Sometimes the challenge isn't turning them on—it's turning them off." When an entrepreneur learns that a product or an approach won't work, it is critical to end the experiment and move in a new direction.

New venture formation will always be fraught with risks. We don't want to imply that a systematic approach to identifying and mitigating them will eliminate them. But we do take issue with the notion that it's the risks that produce the rewards. As Bob Reiss's story has illustrated for decades—and our experience continues to confirm—great entrepreneurs don't take risks; they manage them. Quickly determining what's right

Case Study

ROBIN WOLANER, WHO LAUNCHED *Parenting* magazine, began with an insight: Large numbers of highly educated women were having children much later in their professional careers than had been true in the past. She raised a small amount of seed capital to push her idea for a magazine forward and chose to spend it on answering the one question that, if unresolved, would render all other risks moot: Is there a differentiated need and a real demand for this product? Wolaner sent out direct-response cards describing a magazine that would focus on both parents and would have a uniquely sophisticated editorial orientation. Early market tests typically get a response rate of 3% to 4%. Her cards came back at greater than 7%. Because this deal-killer risk was pulled off the table at the outset, valuation jumped from less than $500,000 to more than $5 million.

and what's wrong with key assumptions and then making speedy adjustments often means the difference between failure and success. As entrepreneurial managers learn to do this, they bend the risk-reward curve in their favor and beat the odds.

CLARK G. GILBERT is the president and CEO of Deseret Digital Media. MATTHEW J. EYRING is the president of Innosight, a strategic innovation consulting and investment company outside Boston.

Originally published in May 2010. Reprint R1005G

Finding Competitive Advantage in Adversity

by Bhaskar Chakravorti

JONATHAN BUSH SAW THE opportunity to dramatically change how obstetrics practices function. He and his partner set out to build a medical business whose objective was to incorporate both traditional and holistic care options for mothers-to-be. Their aspirations were grand, and demand for their services rapidly grew. But when reliance on slow-paying insurers strapped the practice for cash, Bush's vision got tangled in red tape.

In this failure, however, Bush envisioned what would ultimately become his truly innovative business idea: a health care IT service that spares its clients bureaucratic purgatory. That service, athenahealth, is now a $189 million business.

Unlike many managers whose instincts are to hunker down and play it safe during difficult times, entrepreneurs like Bush hear a call to action in the oft-repeated advice of Machiavelli: "Never waste the opportunities offered by a good crisis." Even as the global economy lurches toward a new normal, long-term crises demand solutions in a variety of domains: geopolitics, the environment, health care, education, infrastructure, poverty and inequity juxtaposed with rapid growth, and broken business models in multiple industries. In fact, instead of the waves of expanding frontiers that defined the 20th century, constraint and restraint may define the 21st.

For entrepreneurs with an eye for counterintuitive solutions, extreme problems and seemingly insurmountable adversity can be a crucible for creativity and business-model innovation. In studying hundreds of companies that were created or reinvented in difficult circumstances of many stripes, I have identified four key types of opportunities that innovative entrepreneurs see and seize upon in a climate of extreme adversity. Those who face today's tumultuous business environment can learn from their example. First, let's learn about the business climate of adversity.

Adversity as a Context for Business

Considerable evidence shows that periods of extreme adversity foster innovation and the building of companies. For example, 18 of the 30 firms currently on the Dow Jones Industrial Index were founded during economic downturns. The Kauffman Index of Entrepreneurial Activity showed that the rate of new-business

Idea in Brief

How do some entrepreneurs, corporate innovators, and investors turn adverse conditions to competitive advantage? Chakravorti, of McKinsey and Harvard Business School, has identified four areas that the most successful of these people consistently explore. (1) Entrepreneurs reroute resources that become redundant to meet new needs, as Jonathan Bush did at athenahealth. The company is now a leader in internet-based revenue-cycle management tools. (2) They round up unusual suspects and break industry orthodoxy, as Iqbal Quadir did with Grameenphone in Bangladesh. (3) They find small solutions to big problems, as Trey Moore and Cameron Powell did with their AirStrip OB smartphone app for mobile physicians who needed a major advance in wireless health care. (4) They focus on platform, not just product. That's how Fred Khosravi and Amar Sawhney broadened the field of surgical applications for Incept's hydrogel technology. The entrepreneurs who survive in the "new normal" will be those who find counterintuitive solutions to the bottlenecks, constraints, and other difficulties that adversity engenders. Call them the "new abnormals."

creation was higher during the deepest part of the 2009 recession than it had been in the 14 previous years, including the 1999–2000 technology boom.

Moments of crisis have historically served as a powerful impetus for innovation, whether a Manhattan Project, a moon shot, or industry-transforming "green" consciousness and its related initiatives. The entrepreneurs who thrive in the face of adversity are a different breed from those who flourish when resources are unlimited, such as in Silicon Valley during the 1990s.

What are the factors that distinguish entrepreneurs, corporate innovators, and investors who successfully harness adversity to gain competitive advantage? My research has shown that they tune in to the particular opportunities that characterize challenging times. Unmet need and high entry barriers clearly help to thin out the competitive field, but that's also true for other entrepreneurial circumstances. I instead focus on the opportunities that are unique to situations of adversity and to success in such times. I label the opportunities according to how adversity-attuned entrepreneurs act on them—something they do quickly.

Opportunity 1: Match Unneeded Resources to Unmet Needs

Adversity comes in many forms—acute, cyclical, long-term, and systemic. It sometimes affects individuals or single firms; other times it cuts across a wide swath of entities. However, its pathology is consistent: Adversity constrains a key resource, which then depresses demand, supply, or both. That gives rise to unmet need and releases other resources that become redundant. An opportunity emerges for inventive entrepreneurs who can reroute the redundant resources to fill the unmet need.

Consider, again, Jonathan Bush. He was committed to having an impact in health care, but it didn't happen right away. He drove an ambulance as an EMT, took a break from college to become an army medic after the launch of Operation Desert Storm, and eventually raised $1.6 million (with Todd Park, a former colleague from Booz Allen Hamilton) to buy a San Diego obstetrics practice in 1997.

The partners found that both government and private health insurers would take weeks or months to reimburse the practice, which had little negotiating power, for patients' medical claims. Indeed, physician practices everywhere were struggling with outmoded forms of capturing and storing patient information on paper and Dictaphones. The industry structure and interlocking behaviors across the health care delivery chain had cemented a highly inefficient status quo.

Despite growing revenues, Bush was running out of cash and had to shut down the practice. But he and Park recognized an opportunity in a web-based service, called athenaNet, which they had developed to keep track of patients and their constantly changing insurance information. In 1999, they switched from being a clinical service to deploying athenaNet as a billing tool that would help physicians manage their revenue cycles more efficiently and track changes in insurance rules and provisions. The new company, athenahealth, became a pioneer in revenue-cycle management tools delivered over the internet. It subsequently used its web-based assets to deliver electronic health-records capabilities to its clients and, thereby, also address their need for information efficiency.

The company turned profitable after 2004, when revenues were $36 million, and went on to earn $189 million in 2009. Athenahealth's physician base has grown 30% per year since 2005, with a 97% retention rate. It has the largest, most comprehensive, continually updated database on payer-reimbursement rules—the key drivers of claims payments and denials—in the United Sates. It also has consistently ranked number 1 or 2 in several key ambulatory and billing scheduling categories. Athenahealth stands alone in the field as the only internet-based provider of such services and was named among *Fast Company*'s 50 most innovative businesses for 2010.

Athenahealth ingeniously repurposed a resource made redundant by adverse circumstances to meet a basic need that the adversity had exposed. It's a phenomenon that other sectors have witnessed as well. For example, once-redundant polysilicon has been repurposed by a host of solar energy entrepreneurs. And nascent IT companies in India redeployed plentiful, underutilized, highly trained programmers to respond to the Y2K crisis. Both of these experiences became foundations for the growth of major industries.

Opportunity 2: Round Up Unusual Suspects

Adversity is also characterized by missing or inadequate elements at critical points in the business system. These may include key inputs, capital, technologies, or partners in the supply, distribution, and marketing chains. Entrepreneurs who can creatively identify unlikely, alternative candidates are able to get a leg up. However, the art of aligning the incentives of an unorthodox coalition and maintaining equilibrium among the members is no small challenge.

Some people, such as investment banker Iqbal Quadir, manage to do it. He set out to pursue an outrageous vision: bringing universal telephone service

Adversity: A Disruptive Ingredient for Corporate Innovation

FOR ESTABLISHED COMPANIES, adversity engenders urgency, focus, and an efficient harnessing of resources in the service of innovation and growth. Consider the examples of Cadbury and P&G.

Cadbury in India

Cadbury found opportunity in its predicament as a purveyor of chocolate in the hot climates of southern Asia, where the product melts easily. A new innovation platform was born: Cadbury Bytes and Chocki, added to the familiar Eclairs. Each product has melted chocolate in its core but is not vulnerable to hot outdoor temperatures. The innovations have been very successful in India, and their popularity is spreading globally.

Mr. Clean Car Wash

As the Great Recession of 2008 brought new pressures on P&G, the company allied itself with an unusual list of suspects who had been displaced from their employment and were looking for new businesses to start up. This human resources opportunity coincided with several unmet needs in the market: consumers seeking affordable luxuries in a tough economy, aging Baby Boomers prone to outsourcing services, and communities that value water conservation. The collective result: P&G franchised its 51-year-old Mr. Clean brand to individual car wash entrepreneurs and launched a national chain, Mr. Clean Car Wash. This small entry into service innovation for P&G could lead to other national franchises that leverage P&G's vaunted brands.

to his native Bangladesh, which in 1993 had only one phone per 500 people. One of the world's most resource- and infrastructure-poor countries, Bangladesh also had 80% of its population dispersed across 86,000 villages. Quadir was obviously facing gaps in the supply, distribution, and marketing chain sufficient to kill the best of business plans. How could he possibly implement wireless technology in a cost-efficient way and then market affordable service in this context?

Quadir's real inspiration came when he realized that success would require enlisting the unlikeliest of allies. To benefit from economies of scale, he sought GSM (global system for mobile) digital-wireless technology as the cheapest long-term solution, even though it would be the most expensive at the outset. This took him across the world to Telenor, the Norwegian telecommunications company that is a global leader in GSM.

To scale up sufficiently, Quadir had to solve two additional problems. On the demand side, closing the marketing and distribution gaps meant turning to another unlikely ally, Grameen Bank, the microfinance pioneer that had a deep network among rural women in Bangladesh. Quadir saw an opportunity to repurpose the Grameen business model by encouraging the women to do business in telephones rather than cows and then use the money they made to pay back their microloans from the bank. On the supply side, Quadir had no assurance of interconnection facilities, which would be a barrier to Telenor's attempt to stitch together a nationwide network. To overcome the obstacle, Quadir turned to a third unusual suspect: Bangladesh Railway. The dark fiber along its tracks could be activated to provide the interconnection.

Each player was motivated by the appeal of participating in a new growth opportunity that used existing capacity and technology. Without the simultaneous involvement of the others, however, each ally might have backed away. In effect, the unusual suspects' interlocking incentives had been exquisitely aligned. By orchestrating a counterintuitive coalition, Quadir has made his venture, Grameenphone, the largest telephone provider in Bangladesh today. One in three Bangladeshis now has access to a phone.

Other entrepreneurs have taken different approaches to breaking from industry orthodoxy by seeking out unlikely partners. Take R.P. Eddy, whose clients needed on-the-ground research on hard-to-access markets, such as Iraq. Eddy did not have the capability to send analysts there, so instead he recruited a network of local in-country experts as open-source analysts. The consulting firm, Ergo, was thus born using a radically new model. Alternatively, others have turned to contests and prizes to harness the skills of previously unknown allies to address incredibly tough situations of adversity. According to a recent McKinsey study, the total value of all prizes worth $100,000 or more has grown 15-fold over the past 35 years. Before 1991, 98% of these prizes were for recognition; since then, 78% have been awarded for problem solving.

Opportunity 3: Find Small Solutions to Big Problems

The more severe the adversity, the harder it is to change the status quo. Comprehensive solutions that require many changes can appear to be dead on arrival, leaving only tiny cracks as points of entry to break the mold.

The message for the intrepid entrepreneur: Small innovations can be huge. First, they are potentially more affordable and can be produced with less initial outlay. Second, they economize on features and complexity and may be just good enough to fulfill an unmet need. Third, their size can help minimize environmental effects or other negative externalities. Finally, they may be easier to integrate into the current model, with only minimal adjustments. In fact, four characteristics that, according to Trendwatching.com, define future consumer priorities may be the tiny cracks to look for: affordability, simplicity/convenience, sustainability, and design informed by local knowledge about product usage. Small solutions that fit within these tiny cracks represent major opportunities.

A case in point is Cameron Powell, an obstetrician in San Antonio, Texas, who faced a common problem in his field: potential liability related to failures in communication between the physician and the nursing staff at the expecting mother's bedside. The structural obstacle was that obstetricians are usually on the move—from the office, to the ER, to various hospitals—making continuous bedside coverage cost-prohibitive.

When software engineer Trey Moore asked Powell to wish for his fantasy smartphone application, Powell realized that being able to see the baby's heart tracing and the mother's contractions anytime, anywhere would be a huge help to him and his staff. Powell and Moore figured that avoiding even a single lawsuit, with a median $2.5 million award, could make the investment worthwhile to a health care provider. Together they founded AirStrip Technologies, whose first product was a smartphone app called AirStrip OB. The app was easy to install on devices that physicians were already carrying, required very little behavioral change from users, and would be offered to hospitals on a software-as-a-service model, thereby minimizing their monetary commitment. In short, Powell had found a small solution to a very big problem.

AirStrip OB was celebrated by attendees at the Apple Worldwide Developers Conference in 2009, where only eight apps were chosen to be presented. Since then, more than 100 hospitals have adopted it. Among a highly select handful of inventions in wireless health care, it has been lauded by "rock star cardiologist" Eric Topol and David Pogue, technology columnist for the *New York Times*.

Small innovations such as AirStrip OB aim for major breakthroughs in contexts of extreme adversity. They are not designed simply to make incremental change and are proving to be part of a broad global trend. We now have, for example, cheap and space-efficient sachet packaging of consumer goods in developing markets; microfinance or software-as-a-service to fit limited business budgets; smartphone apps and Twitter for mobile consumers with fragmented attention capacity; and frugally engineered products (from vehicles to appliances to health care items) that ensure affordability and access in the fastest-growing markets, which still face much adversity.

Opportunity 4: Think Platform, Not Just Product

In general, the underlying factors that constrain one situation of adversity also constrain others. This offers an opportunity to invest in a meta-solution that can address several unmet needs simultaneously, either in multiple market segments or various product markets. The multifaceted character of the opportunity also hedges the entrepreneur's risk and helps the venture grow beyond the initial point of entry. Clearly, entrepreneurs can expect varying levels of success, but the broader the venture's reach is, the greater the value to be unlocked. The profit potential comes from the capacity to enhance the business model at three possible leverage points: customer value, cost management, and growth-vector creation.

Fred Khosravi and Amar Sawhney are an excellent example of a team who thought creatively about platform. Described by *In Vivo* as the "dynamic device development duo," these biomedical entrepreneurs banded together to create Incept. They wanted the company to have no physical offices, only two or three employees, and an annual budget of less than $1 million. But Incept was a powerhouse. It held the rights to a "secret sauce" that would be responsible for nine start-ups in 11 years (none of them failed). Of the three spin-offs from these companies, the first, Confluent Surgical, was sold to Covidien for $245 million. The sauce was hydrogel, a harmless and highly versatile biodegradeable polymer.

Sawhney, the inventor of hydrogel technology, foresaw many applications, each solving a dilemma for physicians who performed complex or minimally invasive surgeries in medical specialties as varied as cardiology, gynecology, neurology, and ophthalmology. Current uses now include sealing organs and other parts of the anatomy (such as the lungs, brain, spinal cord, and blood vessels) that are at risk for leakage during surgery. Hydrogels can also be used to separate a damaged organ from an adjacent organ in order to avoid interference with healing.

The duo had clearly tapped into an opportunity with long-term potential for improving surgical procedures. Hydrogel technology was a true platform that could be applied to many parts of the human anatomy and, therefore, in multiple surgical "markets." Ordinarily, venture capitalists and acquiring companies invest in a business whose core technologies are bundled with the products they sell in specific markets. Sawhney and Khosravi resisted convention, however, and focused on keeping the platform—and a stream of applications to address multiple problems—alive. They knew that bundling the hydrogel technology with its application could allow an acquiring company to own it, apply it only in a narrow market segment, and not use its full potential. Instead, they organized Incept so that it would own the patents on the hydrogel technology and license them to independent spin-off companies that Incept would incubate. It was a novel risk-management plan: an entire portfolio of application spin-offs targeting different markets but centered on a common core technology.

The notion of platforms need not be limited, though, to technologies and processes. Consider the case of the performance act Blue Man Group. As artists, they found the 1980s to be a particularly depressing decade. In New York City's Central Park in 1988, they performed "Funeral for the '80s," during which they buried a Rambo doll and a piece of the Berlin Wall. For two decades since that unique debut, they have drummed, splashed paint, caught gumballs with their teeth, and smothered their audiences in toilet paper. The formula for the act was nothing short of a creative mission. Now that they are older and have children, the members of the group have turned their creative attention to another institution they find depressing: primary school education. They founded an alternative elementary school, called the Blue School, predicated on the same mission-driven platform as that of their original entertainment business: "to inspire creativity and connect people with their primal exuberance."

A New Twist on Adverse Selection

To ground your thinking about the benefits that adversity can offer, go back to Michael E. Porter in *The Competitive Advantage of Nations*: "Competitive advantage emerges from pressure, challenge, and adversity, rarely from an easy life." Necessity, coupled with four key opportunities, can indeed be the mother of some serious inventions.

Self-Assessment: Opportunity in Adversity

USE THESE FIVE QUESTIONS to help you unearth the competitive advantage that adversity can offer:

1. What underlying customer needs in your target market are being curtailed by adversity? Have new needs emerged because of the adverse circumstances?

2. Look broadly across your business and in completely unrelated areas. What resources—products, people, materials, technologies, or intellectual property—are being displaced or underutilized because of the adversity?

3. Can you see a way to use resources from your answers to question 2 to fulfill a need you identified in question 1?

4. What is the minimum change that customers or your value chain require to adopt your offering? Then, what subsequent changes are likely, and how far could the adoption spread?

5. Can you repeat your success with questions 1 to 4 in additional markets, such as new customers or new products?

During the 20th century, many breakthroughs took us to uncharted and unimagined territory. But now we are discovering their unintended consequences: unbalanced growth and self-limiting orthodoxies, which may well be the predominant features of the decades ahead. For example, the once-booming high-tech and auto industries are now in search of radically new business models to avoid obsolescence. Widespread discovery and use of nonrenewable resources are revealing their true environmental and geopolitical consequences. Health care innovations bred unsustainable cost structures, demographic imbalances, and limitations in pharmaceutical and health care delivery. Globalization has created myriad challenges of rapid growth in unevenly developed economies (such as Brazil, China, and India) and the potential that regional crises will spread throughout the world. And financial innovations led to uncontrolled speculative bubbles in some sectors. In the past few years alone, we have experienced some of the effects, including the Great Recession and its still-uncertain recovery, an unprecedented crisis with the euro, and the largest accidental oil spill in history. Clearly, the "new normal" is not short on adversity.

None of this will weaken entrepreneurship and innovation. The "new abnormals"—the entrepreneurs who survive—will be those who harness the competitive advantage of adversity. The present century holds a treasure trove of bottlenecks, constraints, and other major difficulties that will be with us for a long time. It would be a shame if—as entrepreneurs, managers, and investors—we were to let such an abundance of serious crises go to waste.

BHASKAR CHAKRAVORTI is a partner at McKinsey & Company and a distinguished scholar at MIT's Legatum Center for Development and Entrepreneurship.

Originally published in November 2010. Reprint R1011H

The Questions Every Entrepreneur Must Answer

by Amar Bhidé

OF THE HUNDREDS OF thousands of business ventures that entrepreneurs launch every year, many never get off the ground. Others fizzle after spectacular rocket starts.

A six-year-old condiment company has attracted loyal customers but has achieved less than $500,000 in sales. The company's gross margins can't cover its overhead or provide adequate incomes for the founder and the family members who participate in the business. Additional growth will require a huge capital infusion, but investors and potential buyers aren't keen on small, marginally profitable ventures, and the family has exhausted its resources.

Another young company, profitable and growing rapidly, imports novelty products from the Far East and sells them to large U.S. chain stores. The founder, who has a paper net worth of several million dollars, has been nominated for entrepreneur-of-the-year awards.

But the company's spectacular growth has forced him to reinvest most of his profits to finance the business's growing inventories and receivables. Furthermore, the company's profitability has attracted competitors and tempted customers to deal directly with the Asian suppliers. If the founder doesn't do something soon, the business will evaporate.

Like most entrepreneurs, the condiment maker and the novelty importer get plenty of confusing counsel: Diversify your product line. Stick to your knitting. Raise capital by selling equity. Don't risk losing control just because things are bad. Delegate. Act decisively. Hire a professional manager. Watch your fixed costs.

Why all the conflicting advice? Because the range of options—and problems—that founders of young businesses confront is vast. The manager of a mature company might ask, What business are we in? or How can we exploit our core competencies? Entrepreneurs must continually ask themselves what business they *want* to be in and what capabilities they would *like* to develop. Similarly, the organizational weaknesses and imperfections that entrepreneurs confront every day would cause the managers of a mature company to panic. Many young enterprises simultaneously lack coherent strategies, competitive strengths, talented employees, adequate controls, and clear reporting relationships.

The entrepreneur can tackle only one or two opportunities and problems at a time. Therefore, just as a parent should focus more on a toddler's motor skills than on his or her social skills, the entrepreneur must distinguish critical issues from normal growing pains.

Idea in Brief

Of the hundreds of thousands of business ventures launched each year, many never get off the ground. Others fizzle after spectacular rocket starts.

Why such dismal odds? Entrepreneurs—with their bias for action—often ignore ingredients essential to business success. These include a clear strategy, the right workforce talent, and organizational controls that spur performance without stifling employees' initiative.

Moreover, no two ventures take the same path. Thus entrepreneurs can't look to formulas to navigate the myriad choices arising as their enterprise evolves. A decision that's right for one venture may prove disastrous for another.

How to chart a successful course for *your* venture? Bhide recommends asking yourself these questions:

- **Where do I want to go?** Consider your goals for the business: Do you want the rush that rapid growth delivers? A chance to experiment with new technology? Capital gains from selling a successful company?

- **How will I get there?** Is your strategy sound? Does it clarify what your company will and won't do? Will it generate sufficient profits and growth?

- **Can I do it?** Do you have the right talent? Reliable sources of capital?

Improvisation takes a venture only so far. *Successful* entrepreneurs keep asking tough questions about where they want to go—and whether the track they're on will take them there.

Entrepreneurs cannot expect the sort of guidance and comfort that an authoritative child-rearing book can offer parents. Human beings pass through physiological and psychological stages in a more or less predetermined order, but companies do not share a developmental path. Microsoft, Lotus, WordPerfect, and Intuit, although competing in the same industry, did not evolve in the same way. Each of those companies has its

Idea in Practice

A closer look at Bhide's three questions.

Where Do I Want to Go?

To articulate your goals for the enterprise, clarify:

- **What you want personally from your business:** An outlet for artistic talent? A flexible lifestyle? The immortality of building an institution that embodies your values? Quick profits?

- **The kind of enterprise required:** For example, if you want to sell your business eventually, you'll need to build a sustainable enterprise—one that can renew itself through changing generations of technology, employees, and customers. And you'll need a company big enough to support an infrastructure that won't require your daily intervention.

- **Your risk tolerance:** For example, building a sustainable business entails risky long-term bets—including trusting inexperienced employees, personally guaranteeing debt, and tolerating delayed payoffs. Are your goals worth the attendant risks?

How Will I Get There?

Successful strategies:

- **Provide clear direction:** Articulate the enterprise's policies, geographic reach, capabilities, and decision-making framework—in concise terms that employees, investors, and customers can understand.

- **Generate sufficient profits and growth:** Ensure that your strategy will produce desired business results. For example, Mothers Work—which sells

own story to tell about the development of strategy and organizational structures and about the evolution of the founder's role in the enterprise.

The options that are appropriate for one entrepreneurial venture may be completely inappropriate for another. Entrepreneurs must make a bewildering number of decisions, and they must make the decisions that maternity clothing to professional women—took off only when its founder revised her strategy from mail order (which generated low profits owing to stiff competition) to retail stores.

- **Serve the enterprise long-term:** Anticipate future market saturation, intensified competition, and major technological change, then ensure that your strategy accommodates those future scenarios.

- **Establish the right growth rate:** Plan for a growth rate that will attract customers and capital without causing excessive stress for you and your employees.

Can I Do It?

A great strategy is worthless unless you can execute it. To do so, you'll need the right:

- **Resources:** Augment your workforce with employees possessing the skills, knowledge, and values needed to implement your strategy. A strong workforce attracts customers and investment capital.

- **Infrastructure:** Establish the organizational systems needed to execute your strategy. For example, suppose you want to build a geographically dispersed business, grow rapidly, and eventually go public. In this case, you'll need to invest heavily in mechanisms for delegating tasks, specializing job roles, forecasting and monitoring availability of funds, and maintaining financial records.

- **Role flexibility:** To grow your business, your role must shift from doing the "real work" to teaching others to do it, prescribing desired results, and managing the work environment.

are right for them. The framework I present here and the accompanying rules of thumb will help entrepreneurs analyze the situations in which they find themselves, establish priorities among the opportunities and problems they face, and make rational decisions about the future. This framework, which is based on my observation of several hundred start-up ventures over eight years, doesn't prescribe answers. Instead, it helps entrepreneurs pose useful questions, identify important issues, and evaluate solutions. The framework applies whether the enterprise is a small printing shop trying to stay in business or a catalog retailer seeking hundreds of millions of dollars in sales. And it works at almost any point in a venture's evolution. Entrepreneurs should use the framework to evaluate their companies' position and trajectory often—not just when problems appear.

The framework consists of a three-step sequence of questions. The first step clarifies entrepreneurs' current goals, the second evaluates their strategies for attaining those goals, and the third helps them assess their capacity to execute their strategies. The hierarchical organization of the questions requires entrepreneurs to confront

An entrepreneur's guide to the big issues

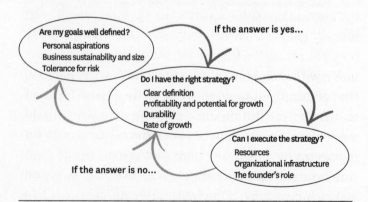

Are my goals well defined?
Personal aspirations
Business sustainability and size
Tolerance for risk

If the answer is yes...

Do I have the right strategy?
Clear definition
Profitability and potential for growth
Durability
Rate of growth

Can I execute the strategy?
Resources
Organizational infrastructure
The founder's role

If the answer is no...

the basic, big-picture issues before they think about refinements and details. (See the exhibit "An entrepreneur's guide to the big issues.") This approach does not assume that all companies—or all entrepreneurs—develop in the same way, so it does not prescribe a one-size-fits-all methodology for success.

Clarifying Goals: Where Do I Want to Go?

An entrepreneur's personal and business goals are inextricably linked. Whereas the manager of a public company has a fiduciary responsibility to maximize value for shareholders, entrepreneurs build their businesses to fulfill personal goals and, if necessary, seek investors with similar goals.

Before they can set goals for a business, entrepreneurs must be explicit about their personal goals. And they must periodically ask themselves if those goals have changed. Many entrepreneurs say that they are launching their businesses to achieve independence and control their destiny, but those goals are too vague. If they stop and think about it, most entrepreneurs can identify goals that are more specific. For example, they may want an outlet for artistic talent, a chance to experiment with new technology, a flexible lifestyle, the rush that comes from rapid growth, or the immortality of building an institution that embodies their deeply held values. Financially, some entrepreneurs are looking for quick profits, some want to generate a satisfactory cash flow, and others seek capital gains from building and selling a company. Some entrepreneurs who want to build sustainable institutions do not consider personal financial returns a high priority. They may refuse acquisition proposals regardless of the price or sell equity cheaply to employees to secure their loyalty to the institution.

Only when entrepreneurs can say what they want personally from their businesses does it make sense for them to ask the following three questions.

What kind of enterprise do I need to build?

Long-term sustainability does not concern entrepreneurs looking for quick profits from in-and-out deals. Similarly, so-called lifestyle entrepreneurs, who are interested only in generating enough of a cash flow to maintain a certain way of life, do not need to build businesses that could survive without them. But sustainability—or the perception thereof—matters greatly to entrepreneurs who hope to sell their businesses eventually. Sustainability is even more important for entrepreneurs who want to build an institution that is capable of renewing itself through changing generations of technology, employees, and customers.

Entrepreneurs' personal goals should also determine the target size of the businesses they launch. A lifestyle entrepreneur's venture needn't grow very large. In fact, a business that becomes too big might prevent the founder from enjoying life or remaining personally involved in all aspects of the work. In contrast, entrepreneurs seeking capital gains must build companies large enough to support an infrastructure that will not require their day-to-day intervention.

What risks and sacrifices does such an enterprise demand?

Building a sustainable business—that is, one whose principal productive asset is not just the founder's skills, contacts, and efforts—often entails making risky long-term bets. Unlike a solo consulting practice—which generates cash from the start—durable ventures, such as companies that produce branded consumer goods, need continued investment to build sustainable advantages. For instance, entrepreneurs may have to advertise to build a brand name. To pay for ad campaigns, they may have to reinvest profits, accept equity partners, or personally guarantee debt. To build depth in their organizations, entrepreneurs may have to trust inexperienced employees to make crucial decisions. Furthermore, many years may pass before any payoff materializes—if it materializes at all. Sustained risk taking can be stressful. As one entrepreneur observes, "When you start, you just do it, like the Nike ad says. You are naïve because you haven't made your mistakes yet. Then you learn about all the things that can go wrong. And because your equity now has value, you feel you have a lot more to lose."

Entrepreneurs who operate small-scale, or lifestyle, ventures face different risks and stresses. Talented people usually avoid companies that offer no stock options and only limited opportunities for personal growth, so the entrepreneur's long hours may never end. Because personal franchises are difficult to sell and often require the owner's daily presence, founders may become locked into their businesses. They may face financial distress if they become sick or just burn out. "I'm always running, running, running," complains one entrepreneur, whose business earns him half a million dollars per year. "I work 14-hour days, and I can't remember the last time I took a vacation. I would like to sell the business, but who wants to buy a company with no infrastructure or employees?"

Can I accept those risks and sacrifices?

Entrepreneurs must reconcile what they want with what they are willing to risk. Consider Joseph Alsop, co-founder and president of Progress Software Corporation. When Alsop launched the company in 1981, he was in his mid-thirties, with a wife and three children. With that responsibility, he says, he didn't want to take the risks necessary to build a multi-billion-dollar corporation like Microsoft, but he and his partners were willing to assume the risks required to build something more than a personal service business. Consequently, they picked a market niche that was large enough to let them build a sustainable company but not so large that it would attract the industry's giants. They worked for two years without salaries and invested their personal savings. In ten years, they had built Progress into a $200 million publicly held company.

Entrepreneurs would do well to follow Alsop's example by thinking explicitly about what they are and are not willing to risk. If entrepreneurs find that their businesses—even if very successful—won't satisfy them personally, or if they discover that achieving their personal goals requires them to take more risks and make more sacrifices than they are willing to, they need to reset their goals. When entrepreneurs have aligned their personal and their business goals, they must then make sure that they have the right strategy.

Setting Strategy: How Will I Get There?

Many entrepreneurs start businesses to seize short-term opportunities without thinking about long-term strategy. Successful entrepreneurs, however, soon make the transition from a tactical to a strategic orientation so that they can begin to build crucial capabilities and resources.

Formulating a sound strategy is more basic to a young company than resolving hiring issues, designing control systems, setting reporting relationships, or defining the founder's role. Ventures based on a good strategy can survive confusion and poor leadership, but sophisticated control systems and organizational structures cannot compensate for an unsound strategy. Entrepreneurs should periodically put their strategies to the following four tests.

Is the strategy well defined?

A company's strategy will fail all other tests if it doesn't provide a clear direction for the enterprise. Even solo entrepreneurs can benefit from a defined strategy. For example, deal makers who specialize in particular industries or types of transactions often have better access to potential deals than generalists do. Similarly, independent consultants can charge higher fees if they have a reputation for expertise in a particular area.

An entrepreneur who wants to build a sustainable company must formulate a bolder and more explicit strategy. The strategy should integrate the entrepreneur's aspirations with specific long-term policies about the needs the company will serve, its geographic reach, its technological capabilities, and other strategic considerations. To help attract people and resources, the strategy must embody the entrepreneur's vision of where the company is going instead of where it is. The strategy must also provide a framework for making the decisions and setting the policies that will take the company there.

The strategy articulated by the founders of Sun Microsystems, for instance, helped them make smart decisions as they developed the company. From the outset, they decided that Sun would forgo the niche-market strategy commonly used by Silicon Valley start-ups. Instead, they elected to compete with industry leaders IBM and Digital by building and marketing a general-purpose workstation. That strategy, recalls cofounder and former president Vinod Khosla, made Sun's product-development choices obvious. "We wouldn't develop any applications software," he explains. This strategy also dictated that Sun assume the risk of building a direct sales force and providing its own field support— just like its much larger competitors. "The Moon or Bust was our motto," Khosla says. The founders' bold vision helped attract premier venture-capital firms and gave Sun extraordinary visibility within its industry.

To be useful, strategy statements should be concise and easily understood by key constituents such as employees, investors, and customers. They must also preclude activities and investments that, although they seem attractive, would deplete the company's resources. A strategy that is so broadly stated that it permits a company to do anything is tantamount to no strategy at all. For instance, claiming to be in the leisure and entertainment business does not preclude a tent manufacturer from operating casinos or making films. Defining the venture as a high-performance outdoor-gear company provides a much more useful focus.

Can the strategy generate sufficient profits and growth?

Once entrepreneurs have formulated clear strategies, they must determine whether those strategies will allow the ventures to be profitable and to grow to a desirable size. The failure to earn satisfactory returns should prompt entrepreneurs to ask tough questions: What's the source, if any, of our competitive edge? Are our offerings really better than our competitors'? If they are, does the premium we can charge justify the additional costs we incur, and can we move enough volume at higher prices to cover our fixed costs? If we are in a commodity business, are our costs lower than our competitors'? Disappointing growth should also raise concerns: Is the market large enough? Do diseconomies of scale make profitable growth impossible?

No amount of hard work can turn a kitten into a lion. When a new venture is faltering, entrepreneurs must address basic economic issues. For instance, many people are attracted to personal service businesses, such as laundries and tax-preparation services, because they can start and operate those businesses just by working hard. They don't have to worry about confronting large competitors, raising a lot of capital, or developing proprietary technology. But the factors that make it easy for entrepreneurs to launch such businesses often prevent them from attaining their long-term goals. Businesses based on an entrepreneur's willingness to work hard usually confront other equally determined competitors. Furthermore, it is difficult to make such companies large enough to support employees and infrastructure. Besides, if employees can do what the founder does, they have little incentive to stay with the venture. Founders of such companies often cannot have the lifestyle they want, no matter how talented they are. With no way to leverage their skills, they can eat only what they kill.

Entrepreneurs who are stuck in ventures that are unprofitable and cannot grow satisfactorily must take radical action. They must find a new industry or develop innovative economies of scale or scope in their existing fields. Rebecca Matthias, for example, started Mothers Work in 1982 to sell maternity clothing to professional women by mail order. Mail-order businesses are easy to start, but with tens of thousands of catalogs vying for consumers' attention, low response rates usually lead to low profitability—a reality that Matthias confronted after three years in the business. In 1985, she borrowed $150,000 to open the first retail store specializing in maternity clothes for working women. By 1994, Mothers Work was operating 175 stores generating about $59 million in revenues.

One alternative to radical action is to stick with the failing venture and hope for the big order that's just around the corner or the greater fool who will buy the business. Both hopes are usually futile. It's best to walk away.

Is the strategy sustainable?

The next issue entrepreneurs must confront is whether their strategies can serve the enterprise over the long term. The issue of sustainability is especially significant for entrepreneurs who have been riding the wave of a new technology, a regulatory change, or any other change—exogenous to the business—that creates situations in which supply cannot keep up with demand. Entrepreneurs who catch a wave can prosper at the outset just because the trend is on their side; they are competing not with one another but with outmoded players. But what happens when the wave crests? As market imbalances disappear, so do many of the erstwhile high fliers who had never developed distinctive capabilities or established defensible competitive positions. Wave riders must anticipate market saturation, intensifying competition, and the next wave. They have to abandon the me-too approach in favor of a new, more durable business model. Or they may be able to sell their high-growth businesses for handsome prices in spite of the dubious long-term prospects.

Consider Edward Rosen, who cofounded Vydec in 1972. The company developed one of the first standalone word processors, and as the market for the machines exploded, Vydec rocketed to $90 million in revenues in its sixth year, with nearly 1,000 employees in the United States and Europe. But Rosen and his partner could see that the days of stand-alone word processors were numbered. They happily accepted an offer from Exxon to buy the company for more than $100 million.

Such forward thinking is an exception. Entrepreneurs in rapidly growing companies often don't consider exit strategies seriously. Encouraged by short-term success, they continue to reinvest profits in unsustainable businesses until all they have left is memories of better days.

Entrepreneurs who start ventures not by catching a wave but by creating their own wave face a different set of challenges in crafting a sustainable strategy. They must build on their initial strength by developing multiple strengths. Brand-new ventures usually cannot afford to innovate on every front. Few start-ups, for example, can expect to attract the resources needed to market a revolutionary product that requires radical advances in technology, a new manufacturing process, and new distribution channels. Cash-strapped entrepreneurs usually focus first on building and exploiting a few sources of uniqueness and use standard, readily available elements in the rest of the business. Michael Dell, the founder of Dell Computer, for example, made low price an option for personal computer buyers by assembling standard components in a college dormitory room and selling by mail order without frills or much sales support.

Strategies for taking the hill, however, won't necessarily hold it. A model based on one or two strengths becomes obsolete as success begets imitation. For instance, competitors can easily knock off an entrepreneur's innovative product. But they will find it much more difficult to replicate systems that incorporate many distinct and complementary capabilities. A business with an attractive product line, well-integrated manufacturing and logistics, close relationships with distributors, a culture of responsiveness to customers, and the capability to produce a continuing stream of product innovations is not easy to copy.

Entrepreneurs who build desirable franchises must quickly find ways to broaden their competitive capabilities. For example, software start-up Intuit's first product, Quicken, had more attractive features and was easier to use than other personal-finance software programs. Intuit realized, however, that competitors could also make their products easy to use, so the company took advantage of its early lead to invest in a variety of strengths. Intuit enhanced its position with distributors by introducing a family of products for small businesses, including QuickBooks, an accounting program. It brought sophisticated marketing techniques to an industry that "viewed customer calls as interruptions to the sacred art of programming," according to the company's founder and chairman, Scott Cook. It established a superior product-design process with multifunctional teams that included marketing and technical support. And Intuit invested heavily to provide customers with outstanding technical support for free.

Are my goals for growth too conservative or too aggressive?

After defining or redefining the business and verifying its basic soundness, an entrepreneur should determine whether plans for its growth are appropriate. Different enterprises can and should grow at different rates. Setting the right pace is as important to a young business as it is to a novice bicyclist. For either one, too fast or too slow can lead to a fall. The optimal growth rate for a fledgling enterprise is a function of many interdependent factors. (See the sidebar "Finding the Right Growth Rate.")

Executing the Strategy: Can I Do It?

The third question entrepreneurs must ask themselves may be the hardest to answer because it requires the most candid self-examination: Can I execute the strategy? Great ideas don't guarantee great performance. Many young companies fail because the entrepreneur can't execute the strategy; for instance, the venture may run out of cash, or the entrepreneur may be unable to generate sales or fill orders. Entrepreneurs must examine three areas—resources, organizational capabilities, and their personal roles—to evaluate their ability to carry out their strategies.

Do I have the right resources and relationships?
The lack of talented employees is often the first obstacle to the successful implementation of a strategy. During the start-up phase, many ventures cannot attract top-notch employees, so the founders perform most of the crucial tasks themselves and recruit whomever they can to help out. After that initial period, entrepreneurs can and should be ambitious in seeking new talent,

especially if they want their businesses to grow quickly. Entrepreneurs who hope that they can turn underqualified and inexperienced employees into star performers eventually reach the conclusion, along with Intuit founder Cook, that "you can't coach height." Moreover, after a venture establishes even a short track record, it can attract a much higher caliber of employee.

In determining how to upgrade the workforce, entrepreneurs must address many complex and sensitive issues: Should I recruit individuals for specific slots or, as is commonly the case in talent-starved organizations, should I create positions for promising candidates? Are the recruits going to manage or replace existing employees? How extensive should the replacements be? Should the replacement process be gradual or quick? Should I, with my personal attachment to the business, make termination decisions myself or should I bring in outsiders?

A young venture needs more than internal resources. Entrepreneurs must also consider their customers and sources of capital. Ventures often start with the customers they can attract the most quickly, which may not be the customers the company eventually needs. Similarly, entrepreneurs who begin by bootstrapping, using money from friends and family or loans from local banks, must often find richer sources of capital to build sustainable businesses.

For a new venture to survive, some resources that initially are external may have to become internal. Many start-ups operate at first as virtual enterprises because the founders cannot afford to produce in-house

Finding the Right Growth Rate

FINDING THE OPTIMAL GROWTH RATE for a new enterprise is a difficult and critical task. To set the right pace, entrepreneurs must consider many factors, including the following.

Economies of Scale, Scope, or Customer Network

The greater the returns to a company's scale, scope, or the size of its customer network, the stronger the case for pursuing rapid growth. When scale causes profitability to increase considerably, growth soon pays for itself. And in industries in which economies of scale or scope limit the number of viable competitors, establishing a favorable economic position first can help deter rivals.

The Ability to Lock In Customers or Scarce Resources

Rapid growth also makes sense if consumers are inclined to stick with the companies with which they initially do business, either because of an aversion to change or because of the expense of switching to another company. Similarly, in retail, growing rapidly can allow a company to secure the most favorable locations or dominate a geographic area that can support only one large store, even if national economies of scale are limited.

Competitors' Growth

If rivals are expanding quickly, a company may be forced to do the same. In markets in which one company generally sets the industry's standard, such as the market for personal-computer operating-system software, growing quickly enough to stay ahead of the pack may be a young company's only hope.

Resource Constraints

A new venture will not be able to grow rapidly if there is a shortage of skilled employees or if investors and lenders are unwilling to fund an expansion that they consider reckless. A venture that is growing quickly, however, will be able to attract capital as well as the employees and customers who want to go with a winner.

Internal Financing Capability

When a new venture is not able to attract investors or borrow at reasonable terms, its internal financing capability will determine the pace at which it can grow. Businesses that have high profit margins and low assets-to-sales ratios can fund high growth rates. A self-funded business, according to the well-known sustainable growth formula, cannot expand its revenues at a rate faster than its return on equity.

Tolerant Customers

When a company is young and growing rapidly, its products and services often contain some flaws. In some markets, such as certain segments of the high-tech industry, customers are accustomed to imperfect offerings and may even derive some pleasure from complaining about them. Companies in such markets can expand quickly. But in markets in which buyers will not stand for breakdowns and bugs, such as the market for luxury goods and mission-critical process-control systems, growth should be much more cautious.

Personal Temperament and Goals

Some entrepreneurs thrive on rapid growth; others are uncomfortable with the crises and fire fighting that usually accompany it. One of the limits on a new venture's growth should be the entrepreneur's tolerance for stress and discomfort.

and hire employees, and because they value flexibility. But the flexibility that comes from owning few resources is a double-edged sword. Just as a young company is free to stop placing orders, suppliers can stop filling them. Furthermore, a company with no assets signals to customers and potential investors that the entrepreneur may not be committed for the long haul. A business with no employees and hard assets may also be difficult to sell, because potential buyers will probably worry that the company will vanish when the founder departs. To build a durable company, an entrepreneur may have to consider integrating vertically or replacing subcontractors with full-time employees.

How strong is the organization?

An organization's capacity to execute its strategy depends on its "hard" infrastructure—its organizational structure and systems—and on its "soft" infrastructure—its culture and norms.

The hard infrastructure an entrepreneurial company needs depends on its goals and strategies. (See the sidebar "Investing in Organizational Infrastructure.") Some entrepreneurs want to build geographically dispersed businesses, realize synergies by sharing resources across business units, establish first-mover advantages through rapid growth, and eventually go public. They must invest more in organizational infrastructure than their counterparts who want to build simple, single-location businesses at a cautious pace.

A venture's growth rate provides an important clue to whether the entrepreneur has invested too much or too little in the company's structure and systems. If performance is sluggish—if, for example, growth lags behind expectations and new products are late—excessive rules and controls may be stifling employees. If, in contrast, the business is growing rapidly and gaining share, inadequate reporting mechanisms and controls are a more likely concern. When a new venture is growing at a fast pace, entrepreneurs must simultaneously give new employees considerable responsibility and monitor their finances very closely. Companies like Blockbuster Video cope by giving frontline employees all the operating autonomy they can handle while maintaining tight, centralized financial controls.

An evolving organization's culture also has a profound influence on how well it can execute its strategy. Culture determines the personalities and temperaments of the workforce; lone wolves are unlikely to want to work in a consensual organization, whereas shy introverts may avoid rowdy outfits. Culture fills in the gaps that an organization's written rules do not anticipate. Culture determines the degree to which individual employees and organizational units compete and cooperate, and how they treat customers. More than any other factor, culture determines whether an organization can cope with the crises and discontinuities of growth.

Unlike organizational structures and systems, which entrepreneurs often copy from other companies, culture must be custom built. As many software makers have found, for instance, a laid-back organization can't compete well against Microsoft. The rambunctiousness

Investing in Organizational Infrastructure

FEW ENTREPRENEURS START OUT with both a well-defined strategy and a plan for developing an organization that can achieve that strategy. In fact, many start-ups, which don't have formal control systems, decision-making processes, or clear roles for employees, can hardly be called organizations. The founders of such ventures improvise. They perform most of the important functions themselves and make decisions as they go along.

Informality is fine as long as entrepreneurs aren't interested in building a large, sustainable business. Once that becomes their goal, however, they must start developing formal systems and processes. Such organizational infrastructure allows a venture to grow, but at the same time, it increases overhead and may slow down decision making. How much infrastructure is enough and how much is too much? To match investments in infrastructure to the requirements of a venture's strategy, entrepreneurs must consider the degree to which their strategy depends on the following.

Delegating Tasks

As a young venture grows, its founders will probably need to delegate many of the tasks that they used to perform. To get employees to perform those tasks competently and diligently, the founders may need to establish mechanisms to monitor employees and standard operating procedures and policies. Consider an extreme example. Randy and Debbi Fields pass along their skills and knowledge through software that tells employees in every Mrs. Fields Cookies shop exactly how to make cookies and operate the business. The software analyzes data such as local weather conditions and the day of the week to generate hourly instructions about such matters as which cookies to bake, when to offer free samples, and when to reorder chocolate chips.

Telling employees how to do their jobs, however, can stifle initiative. Companies that require frontline employees to act quickly and resourcefully might decide to focus more on outcomes than on behavior, using control systems that set performance targets for employees, compare results against objectives, and provide appropriate incentives.

Specializing Tasks

In a small-scale start-up, everyone does a little bit of everything, but as a business grows and tries to achieve economies of scale and scope, employees must be assigned clearly defined roles and grouped into appropriate organizational units. An all-purpose workshop employee, for example, might become a machine tool operator, who is part of a manufacturing unit. Specialized activities need to be integrated by, for example, creating the position of a general manager, who coordinates the manufacturing and marketing functions, or through systems that are designed to measure and reward employees for cross-functional cooperation. Poor integrative mechanisms are why geographic expansion, vertical integration, broadening of product lines, and other strategies to achieve economies of scale and scope often fail.

Mobilizing Funds for Growth

Cash-strapped businesses that are trying to grow need good systems to forecast and monitor the availability of funds. Outside sources of capital such as banks often refuse to advance funds to companies with weak controls and organizational infrastructure.

Creating a Track Record

If entrepreneurs hope to build a company that they can sell, they must start preparing early. Public markets and potential acquirers like to see an extended history of well-kept financial records and controls to reassure them of the soundness of the business.

of a start-up trading operation may scare away the conservative clients the venture wants to attract. A culture that fits a company's strategy, however, can lead to spectacular performance. Physician Sales & Service (PSS), a medical-products distribution company, has grown from $13 million in sales in 1987 to nearly $500 million in 1995, from 5 branches in Florida to 56 branches covering every state in the continental United States, and from 120 employees to 1,800. Like other rapidly growing companies, PSS has tight financial controls. But, venture capitalist Thomas Dickerson says, "PSS would be just another efficiently managed distribution company if it didn't have a corporate culture that is obsessed with meeting customers' needs and maintaining a meritocracy. PSS employees are motivated by the culture to provide unmatched customer service."

When entrepreneurs neglect to articulate organizational norms and instead hire employees mainly for their technical skills and credentials, their organizations develop a culture by chance rather than by design. The personalities and values of the first wave of employees shape a culture that may not serve the founders' goals and strategies. Once a culture is established, it is difficult to change.

Can I play my role?

Entrepreneurs who aspire to operate small enterprises in which they perform all crucial tasks never have to change their roles. In personal service companies, for instance, the founding partners often perform client work from the time they start the company until they retire. Transforming a fledgling enterprise into an entity capable of an independent existence, however, requires founders to undertake new roles.

Founders cannot build self-sustaining organizations simply by "letting go." Before entrepreneurs have the option of doing less, they first must do much more. If the business model is not sustainable, they must create a new one. To secure the resources demanded by an ambitious strategy, they must manage the perceptions of the resource providers: potential customers, employees, and investors. To build an enterprise that will be able to function without them, entrepreneurs must design the organization's structure and systems and mold its culture and character.

While they are sketching out an expansive view of the future, entrepreneurs also have to manage as if the company were on the verge of going under, keeping a firm grip on expenses and monitoring performance. They have to inspire and coach employees while dealing with the unpleasantness of firing those who will not be able to grow with the company. Bill Nussey, cofounder of the software maker Da Vinci Systems Corporation, recalls that firing employees who had "struggled and cried and sacrificed with the company" was the hardest thing he ever had to do.

Few successful entrepreneurs ever come to play a purely visionary role in their organizations. They remain deeply engaged in what Abraham Zaleznik, the Konosuke Matsushita Professor of Leadership Emeritus at the Harvard Business School, calls the "real work" of their enterprises. Marvin Bower, the founding partner of McKinsey & Company, continued to negotiate and direct studies for clients while leading the firm through a considerable expansion of its size and geographic reach. Bill Gates, co-founder and CEO of multibillion-dollar software powerhouse Microsoft, reportedly still reviews the code that programmers write.

But founders' roles must change. Gates no longer *writes* programs. Michael Roberts, an expert on entrepreneurship, suggests that an entrepreneur's role should evolve from doing the work, to teaching others how to do it, to prescribing desired results, and eventually to managing the overall context in which the work is done. One entrepreneur speaks of changing from quarterback to coach. Whatever the metaphor, the idea is that leaders seek ever increasing impact from what they do. They achieve this by, for example, focusing more on formulating marketing strategies than on selling; negotiating and reviewing budgets rather than directly supervising work; designing incentive plans rather than setting the compensation of individual employees; negotiating the acquisitions of companies instead of the cost of office supplies; and developing a common purpose and organizational norms rather than moving a product out the door.

In evaluating their personal roles, therefore, entrepreneurs should ask themselves whether they continually experiment with new jobs and responsibilities. Founders who simply spend more hours performing the same tasks and making the same decisions as the business grows end up hindering growth. They should ask themselves whether they have acquired any new skills recently. An entrepreneur who is an engineer, for example, might master financial analysis. If founders can't point to new skills, they are probably in a rut and their roles aren't evolving.

Entrepreneurs must ask themselves whether they actually want to change and learn. People who enjoy taking on new challenges and acquiring new skills—Bill Gates, again—can lead a venture from the start-up stage to market dominance. But some people, such as H. Wayne Huizenga, the moving spirit behind Waste Management and Blockbuster Video, are much happier moving on to get other ventures off the ground. Entrepreneurs have a responsibility to themselves and to the people who depend on them to understand what fulfills and frustrates them personally.

Many great enterprises spring from modest, improvised beginnings. William Hewlett and David Packard tried to craft a bowling alley foot-fault indicator and a harmonica tuner before developing their first successful product, an audio oscillator. Wal-Mart Stores' founder, Sam Walton, started by buying what he called a "real dog" of a franchised variety store in Newport, Arkansas, because his wife wanted to live in a small town. Speedy response and trial and error were more important to those companies at the start-up stage than foresight and planning. But pure improvisation—or luck—rarely yields long-term success. Hewlett-Packard might still be an obscure outfit if its founders had not eventually made conscious decisions about product lines, technological capabilities, debt policies, and organizational norms.

Entrepreneurs, with their powerful bias for action, often avoid thinking about the big issues of goals, strategies, and capabilities. They must, sooner or later, consciously structure such inquiry into their companies and their lives. Lasting success requires entrepreneurs to keep asking tough questions about where they want to go and whether the track they are on will take them there.

AMAR BHIDÉ teaches entrepreneurship at Harvard Business School.

Originally published in November 1996. Reprint 96603

Making Social Ventures Work

*by James D. Thompson and
Ian C. MacMillan*

IN RECENT YEARS, we've all experienced considerable volatility—financial breakdowns, natural disasters, wars, and other disruptions. It's clear we need new approaches to the world's toughest economic challenges and social problems. Entrepreneurs can play a central role in finding the solutions, driving economic growth (building infrastructure, developing local talent, infusing struggling regions with investment capital) and helping hundreds of millions of people worldwide. If successful, socially minded entrepreneurial efforts create a virtuous cycle: The greater the profits these ventures make, the greater the incentives for them to grow their businesses. And the more societal problems they help alleviate, the more people who can join the mainstream of global consumers.

The failure rates for new companies and markets, however, are high. That is true anywhere in the world, including emerging economies. The management challenges associated with producing and marketing goods and services at the base of the economic pyramid include imperfect markets, uncertain prices and costs, nonexistent or unreliable infrastructure, weak or totally absent formal governance, untested applications of technology, and unpredictable competitive responses. Given this daunting uncertainty, entrepreneurs need a framework for "unfolding" success from a perceived or an emergent opportunity.

Entrepreneurs and others who want to launch businesses in, say, Latin America, Asia, or Africa but lack reliable data about those environments need to put together the best models and mechanisms they can, documenting their assumptions as they go. Critically, however, they need to systematically test each of the assumptions underpinning their preliminary models against a series of checkpoints and be prepared to change on the fly, redirecting their efforts through a process known as *discovery-driven planning.* In this way, they can act on emerging evidence instead of obstinately and blindly pursuing infeasible objectives. (See Rita Gunther McGrath and Ian C. MacMillan's "Discovery-Driven Planning," HBR July–August 1995.)

However, this method of planning is necessary but not sufficient to handle high-uncertainty ventures. In the following pages, we'll look at how to combine discovery-driven planning with four other guidelines for building successful businesses in uncertain markets that we developed during a sustained field program carried out by the Wharton Societal Wealth Program (WSWP). Specifically, we'll consider four social enterprise projects we

Idea in Brief

Entrepreneurs can play a central role in finding solutions to the world's toughest social problems. The failure rate for start-ups, however, is high. And new ventures in emerging economies face such challenges as uncertain prices and costs, nonexistent or unreliable infrastructure, and unpredictable competitive responses. The authors offer guidelines for launching successful businesses in uncertain markets. One of those guidelines, discovery-driven planning (a well-known process developed by MacMillan and Rita Gunther McGrath), helps managers test their assumptions about preliminary business models and revise them on the basis of emerging data. The remainder were informed by the authors' efforts, with the Wharton Societal Wealth Program, to help launch socially beneficial ventures in Africa and the United States. Those guidelines include outlining the minimum number of people a venture should serve and the minimum level of profitability it should achieve; identifying important stakeholders; planning how to terminate the venture in an acceptable manner; and anticipating unintended consequences of the enterprise. The lessons aren't just for entrepreneurs. The management teams of multinationals, foundations, and NGOs can apply them to any challenging and highly uncertain business situation. In doing so, they can better control their costs, minimize the effects of surprises, and increase their impact on society.

helped launch in Africa and examine how the guidelines informed the work in each.

It's important to note that the lessons here aren't just for entrepreneurs. The management teams of established multinationals, foundations, large NGOs, and other nonprofits can apply them in any challenging and highly uncertain business situation. In doing so, they can better control their costs, increase their impact on society, minimize the effects of surprises, and know when to disengage from questionable projects.

Lessons from the Field

As part of our research in the WSWP—a nine-year-old field research program at the University of Pennsylvania's Wharton School of Business intended to examine the use of business models to develop projects that attack societal problems—we worked with 10 groups of local entrepreneurs trying to launch base-of-the-pyramid ventures in the United States and several African countries. Each project faced some or all of the elements of uncertainty cited earlier. In a few instances, even the initial objectives and desired outcomes were unclear, which made it tougher to make decisions about where and how to allocate resources.

We and our student teams worked with each venture, reviewing socioeconomic and political factors as well as market and competitive conditions, conducting interviews with project participants, and observing and documenting their operations. We helped the entrepreneurs establish strategic partnerships where appropriate, develop business plans, and deploy relevant technologies. Our insights from the fieldwork have been distilled into the following guidelines for creating new business models in emerging or other highly uncertain markets.

1. Define the ballpark—or the scope of the venture.

This is a three-part process. First, concretely *outline the disqualifying conditions,* the factors that would preclude the venture's launch. These might include an inability to scale operations, an environment in which corruption is rampant and can't be circumvented, situations in which the necessary equipment is of poor quality and is difficult to operate and repair, and a lack or shortage of suitable talent. Second, *define your acceptability space:* the minimum number of people the venture should serve and the minimum level of profitability it should attain. And third, after a thorough review of the economic, national, and cultural contexts in which the venture will operate, *draw up the business's rules of engagement.* These might include tenets such as "no sales on credit," "no transgressions of home or host country laws," or "absolutely no payments of bribes." All three filters will help you allocate scarce resources only to ventures that satisfy minimally acceptable outcomes.

2. Attend to the sociopolitics.

Before you even start, you must develop a fine-grained view of important stakeholders, their roles, and the resources they can provide. Identify *beneficiaries*—the (often reluctant) parties who stand to gain from the venture but could nonetheless be initially skeptical of it; *potential allies*—those most likely to support the project; *needed indifferents*—those unlikely to care much about the project but whose support may be critical; and *meaningful opponents*—those who will be adversely affected by the success of the project and have the wherewithal to obstruct it. With such an analysis in hand, you can figure out how best to mobilize supporters and neutralize opponents.

3. Emphasize discovery-driven planning.

From the get-go, recognize the evolving nature of your project. Of course, you must delineate the initial business model, the delivery mechanisms, and the value proposition for customers. But you're probably going to be wrong. The idea is to start with a clearly hypothesized model for the venture, launch it at the lowest possible cost, and use the business data that emerge to continuously update your assumptions, systematically learning your way to the eventual solution.

First, *specify both the unit of business and the unit of benefit.* The unit of business is the transaction unit for which the customer pays—for example, a sack of grain, an hour of service, or a load of materials hauled. The unit of benefit is the metric by which societal impact will be measured—for example, a daily protein serving, a patient treated, or a person taught to read a simple book. There may be few precedents on which to base your assumptions about those factors, but developing and specifying initial assumptions will help you articulate your business and revenue models. Make sure to document your hypotheses and delineate a series of checkpoints at which you'll test them before making major investments in the venture.

Second, *anticipate the challenges of growth.* One of the biggest obstacles to scaling up ventures in emerging economies, for instance, is the shortage of management talent and expertise. It's difficult to attract experienced employees and partners (or even high-potential candidates for education and training) to an uncertain venture.

This limitation alone can seriously undermine aggressive growth plans.

4. Plan disengagement.

There is more than just financial capital at stake in societal-wealth-generating initiatives; the livelihoods and well-being of hundreds, if not thousands, of people also hang in the balance. Before you begin, you must plan how you could disengage with a minimal footprint. How could you exit in an acceptable manner? Could you sell off or donate equipment or other assets? Could you shut down until conditions (say, access to electricity) improve?

5. Try to anticipate unintended consequences.

Recognize that societal interventions (and, in fact, any form of commercial intrusion) in emerging markets can create *unintended second-order effects,* both negative and positive. For instance, when various NGOs and governments encouraged intensive growth in shrimp farming in order to bolster local economies and create new export markets, mangrove forests in parts of Thailand and China were decimated.

Putting the Guidelines to Work

These five guidelines can be applied to *any* new-market-creation challenges—for instance, finding markets for radically new technologies such as nanotechnology, or developing submarkets (such as Chinese and Indian

Turning Uncertainty into Risk

THE DISCOVERY-DRIVEN PROCESS of transforming the uncertainty around a business venture into risk (which can be managed) allows leaders to experiment, learn, and either develop a plausible business model or abandon the project early and at little cost. The idea is to reduce uncertainty to the point where probability distributions can be assigned to expected outcomes, making them plannable—that is, you develop ideas to the point where it's possible to use conventional methods of assessing risk. When you simply don't know what will happen, when there are as many possible answers as there are questions, there's a big opportunity for effectuation—that is, for just starting something inexpensively, for taking some sort of action that has an outcome. By analyzing these preliminary results, you can then further develop your ideas, monitor your progress, and exploit the evolution of any plausible model that emerges.

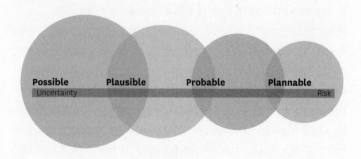

teenagers) in rapidly growing economies. Let's look at four of the 10 Wharton projects and see which guidelines were particularly germane in the case of a venture that has been very successful, one that has been only marginally so, one for which the jury is still out, and one that has been discontinued.

Success: The Feeds Project

The goal of this venture was to produce high-quality, low-cost animal feed in northwest Zambia so that small-scale chicken farmers could generate food for themselves and income from the sale of surplus chickens at competitive prices. The region, known for its copper production, faced staggering levels of unemployment in the 1980s and 1990s, after several mines were shut down. This led to severe malnutrition; many people were close to starvation. The leaders of the Feeds Project started small: Six men, working in a shed, used shovels to mix the feed (a combination of corn, soya, minerals, and other nutrients). The plan was to distribute it through centers affiliated with a large, well-established corporate group. Here's how the Feeds Project applied several of the guidelines:

Scope. The project sought to increase regional consumption of chicken meat by at least 1 million servings per year and to generate a return on sales of animal feed (the bulk of which was for poultry) of at least 12% within three years. The venture would sell its feed for cash, not credit. Initially, it could not poach customers from established regional competitors, nor could it purchase any assets before demonstrating proof of concept. Harsh terms, perhaps, but they acknowledged the difficulties of doing business in a region where bad debt was rampant and uncollectible, and established competitors responded to threats with drastic price-cutting.

Sociopolitics. Many small-scale farmers had little confidence in their ability to raise chickens profitably. So,

What Is Discovery-Driven Planning?

DISCOVERY-DRIVEN PLANNING IS a practical tool (introduced in 1995 HBR article by Rita Gunther McGrath and Ian C. MacMillan) that acknowledges the difference between planning for a new venture and for a more conventional line of business. It recognizes that at the start of a venture, little is known and much is assumed. When new data are uncovered, they are incorporated into the evolving plan. The real potential of the venture is discovered as it develops. With conventional planning, managers can (fairly accurately) extrapolate future results from a platform of past experience. Deviations from plan are considered a bad thing. By contrast, new ventures call for entrepreneurs to envision what is uncertain and not yet obvious to the competition. They must make do with assumptions; and because these assumptions generally turn out to be wrong, new ventures inevitably experience (often huge) deviations from original targets. Entrepreneurs must establish checkpoints at which they convert assumptions into firmer knowledge before making major investments.

with cooperation from leaders in each village, the lead entrepreneur of the project designed an education program to convince these potential beneficiaries of the viability of chicken farming. Going from village to village, she held simple but powerful seminars in which she explained possible financial outcomes and discussed which types of poultry to breed and how to prevent disease. Only then did new growers begin buying the feed.

Discovery. The local entrepreneurs initially assumed that farmers would buy feed by the sack; however, many customers lacked easy access to affordable transportation and needed enough feed for six to eight weeks (a production cycle) at a time. So the venture leaders updated their distribution system accordingly. As demand grew, they expanded their operations and product offerings, first by salvaging discarded equipment and then by purchasing new equipment that could churn out more than 2,000 tons of feed per month, including high-quality poultry pellets.

Second-order effects. The project is generating negative and positive second-order effects. One rather bizarre outcome: As the plant expands to fulfill the demand for more feed for ever-more chickens, communities have to deal with an excess of chicken feathers. There is currently no way to recycle them, and demand for cushions and comforters in a poor, tropical society is limited. So the entrepreneur is developing a furnace for the feathers. Still, positive effects abound: Hundreds have entered the chicken-farming market, many of them hiring as they expand. The greater efficiency of the feed market has led to greater investment: New hatcheries and processing facilities are being built across the region. Several churches are attempting to establish community-based poultry programs in remote areas, and a new market for product sales has opened up in a neighboring country, where the project is already negotiating to develop a feed manufacturing plant.

The Feeds Project, initially created for small poultry breeders, selling for cash in local markets, is now supplying larger commercial poultry growers, mining kitchens, and retail chain stores. It offers broader product lines (such as different size bags and life-cycle-stage formulations) as well as feed for other species, such as dogs and dairy cattle. The path to scaling the business has been through higher-quality machinery, expanded distribution, and moves into adjacent markets.

Marginal Success: The Cookie Project

Huge numbers of uneducated, unmarried mothers in South Africa eke out a precarious living, barely able to feed their children. The Cookie Project was conceived in 2004 to train such women to operate bakeries in distressed areas, making high-quality cookies (using natural ingredients) for health-conscious consumers throughout the country.

The pilot site was in the township of Mfuleni; the lead entrepreneur launched it there because she found a small facility, donated to the township by a wealthy woman from Europe, that had electricity, running water (but no hot water), and, most important, three working ovens. The entrepreneur "leased" the facility from the community, rent-free, in exchange for training and jobs for local women. The company has now relocated to a larger plant. The next step will be to replicate the operation, first in other parts of Africa and then in India and Latin America—but only if the business model can be proven to deliver investment-grade profitability. The entrepreneur has calculated the sales required to create new jobs (building in the cost of training each employee). Here are some guidelines the team used to achieve early success:

Scope. The acceptability space the lead entrepreneur set for the project included training and employing a minimum of 300 so-called unemployables. Apart from learning how to produce cookies, the women were also trained in basic life skills, such as household budgeting and personal hygiene. The venture also set a financial goal: to earn $100,000 in profits in South Africa in the third year of operations.

Sociopolitics. Potential employees had been so beaten down by their adverse circumstances that they had to be convinced that they could, in fact, find gainful work without being exploited. And uninvolved but influential members of the community initially resisted the project for fear that it would decrease their influence. A local elder, for instance, thought that the venture was making too much money, thus undermining her position. (She had no concept of net profits—she just saw hundreds of cases of cookies going out the door.) She and other elders demanded a large fee from the project to continue using the community building. The entrepreneur (and the employees) spent considerable time talking with the elders, explaining the project's profit challenges, broader goals, and the resulting expansion of the local economic base.

Discovery. The original business model was sales of home-style cookies to local distributors. These days, however, the Cookie Project has access to sophisticated food scientists, uses best-in-class ingredients, and exports its products to the United States. It also employs men and women on both sides of the Atlantic.

The financial challenge remains; building a new food brand in the current economic climate is tough. If the venture fails to come up with a profitable distribution model, it may need to redirect its strategy toward e-commerce in order to reduce its marketing costs and extend the lifespan of its current investments.

Disengagement. The lead entrepreneur of the Cookie Project decided that even if the project proved untenable, at the very least it would have considerably enhanced the employability of its workers. They would know, for example, how to read a basic invoice, write checks, and manage customers. Each woman was treated as an entrepreneur in her own right, responsible for her own recipe. For instance, the company charged one worker with figuring out ways to improve the taste, look, quality, and packaging of a particular type of cookie. She "owned" that recipe. The lead entrepreneur also helped guarantee the workers' employment in the event that she had to sell the business: As a condition of sale, the new owners would be required to hire all existing employees.

The Jury's Still Out: The EMR Project

One of the biggest constraints in addressing pandemics in resource-poor environments is the scarcity of physicians. Botswana is a case in point. Its population is being hollowed out by AIDS-related deaths in the economically active 18-to-50 age group. The EMR Project set out to develop an electronic medical records (EMR) system that would help improve patient care. Eventually, the entrepreneurs thought, the system could alleviate the unbearable workload of the country's physicians by allowing nurses to diagnose conditions and prescribe medications for stable patients, consulting doctors only when necessary. The following guidelines were most relevant to this project:

Scope. The venture managers wanted to make at least $80,000 in profits per year and increase the length and improve the quality of life of at least 20,000 patients for at least eight years. With these goals in mind, the project initially trained four nurses to use the EMR system at a pilot site, with an eye toward expanding to at least 70 nurses nationwide. The leaders of the initiative adopted several nonnegotiable rules of engagement. First, high-quality patient care was the number one priority; typical health markers in AIDS patients (such as viral load and CD4 counts) were to be used as measures of quality. Second, patient confidentiality was to be upheld. And third, the project had to comply with the health care laws of both Botswana and the United States.

Discovery. The first hypothesized unit of business was a suite of reports containing clinical data that could be purchased by pharmaceutical companies conducting AIDS research in Botswana. The reports would contain anonymous data from patients who had opted in to the project. The research, it was hoped, would yield improvements in preventive and palliative care. As the venture unfolded, however, it became clear that the pilot site was too small for large research projects; and negotiating multiple patient privacy protocols was too complex at such an early stage. So the primary unit of business became an annual software license contract for clinics and health insurance providers interested in using the EMR system's data to improve their client management and claims processes. Instead of trying to launch a major nationwide program with full EMR and diagnostic capabilities, the project focused on a single private clinic (the largest) and started to build records for 16,000 patients.

Disengagement. The EMR Project gives patients and caregivers access to information about real-time physiological responses to treatment and non-adherence to treatment. So the venture pledged to do no harm: If it needs to exit the market, it will help to maintain this reporting and diagnostic capability by identifying an EMR with similar capabilities and transferring all patient data to its system.

The EMR Project has undergone a number of deliberate redirections, precisely because its leaders haven't figured out how to alleviate the fallout from AIDS and HIV-related illnesses while generating profits from any of their business model revisions. They have been able to continue probing for solutions at a relatively low cost, however: One redirection occurred when patients overwhelmingly said they wanted the same visual aids the physicians used: charts showing the rise and fall of their health markers according to whether they took their medications. This request led to a study to determine whether text messages reminding patients to refill their prescriptions and attend regular consultations with their doctors would increase their adherence to drug regimens and scheduled clinic visits.

The data are currently under analysis. Should text messaging prove effective, the next steps would be to determine the impact of increased adherence on important patient outcomes. If such a study demonstrated positive effects on patient health, the text message reminders could become a component of the EMR business model. However, if the study showed little or no impact on patient adherence and outcomes, and if no sustainable revenue model can be found, the project could be terminated.

The Plug's Been Pulled: The Peanut Project

Peanuts, in combination with milk, can fulfill about 90% of a person's nutritional requirements. But shelling peanuts by hand is arduous, and the cost of modern peanut-shelling equipment is prohibitive for most small-scale producers. The initial concept of the Peanut Project was to encourage relatively isolated rural communities in Africa to grow nuts in order to supply local entrepreneurs who would build small, low-cost plants to process the crops, improving the local distribution of peanuts. In the event of success, a proposed extension of the program was to increase production of the nuts and export them to higher-value customers in more-central locations, such as South Africa. The following guidelines were crucial in assessing the project's viability:

Scope. To determine if its efforts would be worthwhile, the venture defined its scope according to a minimum number of tons of peanuts to be processed and jobs to be created relative to a minimum net profit of $75,000. The project also set the following rules: Secure a safe central processing center. Obtain permissions and authorizations from the local chiefs and village heads. And retain a full-time entrepreneur with the local agricultural experience and skills required to build and manage a processing plant and oversee a network of growers.

Sociopolitics. For rural farmers accustomed to being in control of existing crops and using stored produce to generate cash as needed, the idea of harvesting and then giving up their crops to a third party for processing was hugely suspect. Furthermore, in many rural areas of Africa, arable land is assigned by chiefs or village leaders to growers they deem worthy. The lead entrepreneur quickly understood that he would need buy-in from these elders before the project could launch.

Discovery. The envisaged business model and path to scale for the Peanut Project resembled that of the Feeds Project. In the peanut-processing case, however, a critical driver of success was the management of product "shrinkage" across the logistics chain. Discovery-driven planning showed that a loss of as little as 5% would compromise the likelihood of generating the minimum net profit. The second most influential driver was the transportation of peanuts to the processing facility and then to market. Given the scarcity of trucks, poor roads, and high fuel prices, even the best product was unlikely to capture a high enough price for the growers to compete. These practical realities invalidated the early-stage assumptions. The entrepreneurs were unable to design a system to cope with them or to redirect the project in a way that would attract management know-how. Reluctantly, the venture leaders terminated the project.

Taken together, the five guidelines we've derived from our fieldwork offer an effective framework for *all* organizations—not just entrepreneurs and social enterprises—seeking to create radically new and profitable markets. Large, incumbent organizations and startups alike can use them to create markets for their products. Nonprofits, NGOs, and foundations with limited resources can improve their odds of affecting society in the ways they intend. The discipline engendered by these guidelines—you'll necessarily come back to the framework again and again as your business evolves—will ensure that you maximize limited resources in pursuit of your goals.

JAMES D. THOMPSON teaches innovation, entrepreneurship, and corporate growth at the University of Pennsylvania's Wharton School. **IAN C. MacMILLAN** is the Dhirubhai Ambani Professor of Innovation and Entrepreneurship at the Wharton School.

Originally published in September 2010. Reprint R1009D

The Global Entrepreneur

by Daniel J. Isenberg

FOR A CENTURY AND MORE, companies have ventured abroad only after establishing themselves at home. Moreover, when they have looked overseas, they haven't ventured too far afield, initially. Consumer health care company Johnson & Johnson set up its first foreign subsidiary in Montreal in 1919—33 years after its founding in 1886. Sony, established in 1946, took 11 years to export its first product to the United States, the TR-63 transistor radio. The Gap, founded in 1969—the year Neil Armstrong walked on the moon—opened its first overseas store in London in 1987, a year after the *Challenger* space shuttle disaster.

Companies are being born global today, by contrast. Entrepreneurs don't automatically buy raw materials from nearby suppliers or set up factories close to their headquarters. They hunt for the planet's best manufacturing locations because political and economic barriers have fallen and vast quantities of information are at their fingertips. They also scout for talent across the globe, tap investors wherever they may be located, and learn to manage operations from a distance—the moment they go into business.

Take Bento Koike, who set up Tecsis to manufacture wind turbine blades in 1995. The company imports raw materials from North America and Europe, and its customers are located on those two continents. Yet Koike created his globe-girding start-up near São Paulo in his native Brazil because a sophisticated aerospace industry had emerged there, which enabled him to develop innovative blade designs and manufacturing know-how. Tecsis has become one of the world's market leaders, having installed 12,000 blades in 10 countries in the past decade and racked up revenues of $350 million in 2007.

Standing conventional theory on its head, start-ups now do business in many countries before dominating their home markets. In late 2001, Ron Zwanziger, David Scott, and Jerry McAleer teamed up to launch their third medical diagnostics business, even though Zwanziger lives in the United States and Scott and McAleer live in England. They started Inverness Medical Innovations by retaining the pieces of their company that Johnson & Johnson didn't acquire and immediately gained a presence in Belgium, Germany, Ireland, Israel, the United Kingdom, and the United States. The troika didn't skip a beat. In seven years, they wanted to grow the new venture into an enterprise valued at $7 billion and believed that being born global was the way to do it. They're getting there: Inverness Medical's assets were valued at $5 billion as of August 2008.

Idea in Brief

For over a century, start-ups began by focusing on their home markets. More and more, however, are now being born global—chasing opportunities created by distance, learning to manage faraway operations, and hunting for the planet's best manufacturing locations, brightest talent, most willing investors, and most profitable customers wherever they may be—from day one. That's not easy. In his research, Harvard professor Isenberg has found that global start-ups face three challenges. First are the logistical problems and psychic barriers created by distance and by differences in culture, language, education systems, religion, and economic development levels. Even something so basic as accommodating the world's various workweek schedules can put a strain on a small start-up's staff. Second is

managing the challenges (and opportunities) of context—that is, the different nations' political, regulatory, judicial, tax, and labor environments. Third, like all new ventures, global start-ups must find a way to compete with bigger incumbents while using far fewer resources. To succeed, Isenberg has found, global entrepreneurs must cultivate four competencies: They must clearly articulate their reasons for going global, learn to build alliances with more powerful partners, excel at international supply chain management, and create a multinational culture within their organization. Entrepreneurs shouldn't fear the fact that the world isn't flat. Being global may not be a pursuit for the fainthearted, but even start-ups can thrive by using distance to gain competitive advantage.

Today's entrepreneurs cross borders for two reasons. One is defensive: To be competitive, many ventures, like Tecsis and Inverness Medical, have to globalize some aspects of their business—manufacturing, service delivery, capital sourcing, or talent acquisition, for instance—the moment they start up. That may sound obvious today, but until a few years ago, it was standard practice for U.S. venture capitalists, in particular, to require that the companies they invested in focus on domestic markets.

The other reason is to take the offense. Many new ventures are discovering that a new business opportunity spans more than one country or that they can use distance to create new products or services. Take RacingThePlanet, which Mary Gadams founded in 2002 to stage marathons, each 250 kilometers long and lasting seven days, in the world's most hostile environments. Her team works out of a small Hong Kong office, but the company operates in the Gobi Desert in Mongolia, the Atacama Desert in Chile, the Sahara Desert in Egypt, and Antarctica. Distance has generated the opportunity: If the deserts were accessible, participants and audiences would find the races less attractive, and the brand would be diluted. RacingThePlanet isn't just about running; it's also about creating a global lifestyle brand, which Gadams uses to sell backpacks, emergency supplies, clothing, and other merchandise, as well as to generate content for the multimedia division, which sells video for websites and GPS mapping systems. The company may be just six years old, but brand awareness is high, and RacingThePlanet is already profitable.

In this article, I'll describe the challenges start-ups face when they are born global and the skills entrepreneurs need to tackle them.

Key Challenges

Global entrepreneurs, my research shows, face three distinct challenges.

Distance

New ventures usually lack the infrastructure to cope with dispersed operations and faraway markets. Moreover, physical distances create time differences, which can be remarkably tough to navigate. Even dealing with various countries' workweeks takes a toll on a start-up's limited staff: In North America, Europe, China, and India, corporate offices generally operate Monday through Friday. In Israel, they're open Sunday through Thursday. In Saudi Arabia and the UAE, the workweek runs Saturday through Wednesday, but in other predominantly Muslim countries like Lebanon, Morocco, and Turkey, people work from Monday through Friday or Saturday.

A greater challenge for global entrepreneurs is bridging what the British economist Wilfred Beckerman called in 1956 "psychic distance." This arises from such factors as culture, language, education systems, political systems, religion, and economic development levels. It can heighten—or reduce—psychological barriers between regions and often prompt entrepreneurs to make counterintuitive choices. Take the case of Encantos de Puerto Rico, set up in 1998 to manufacture and market premium Puerto Rican coffee. When founder-CEO Angel Santiago sought new markets in 2002, he didn't enter the nearby U.S. market but chose Spain instead. That's because, he felt, Puerto Ricans and Spaniards have similar tastes in coffee and because of the ease of doing business in Spanish, which reduced the psychic distance between the two countries. When two years later, Encantos de Puerto Rico did enter the United States, it focused initially on Miami, which has a large Hispanic population.

Context

Nations' political, regulatory, judicial, tax, environmental, and labor systems vary. The choices entrepreneurs make about, say, where to locate their companies' headquarters will affect shareholder returns and also their ability to raise capital. When the husband-and-wife team of Andrew Prihodko, a Ukrainian studying at MIT, and Sharon Peyer, a Swiss-American citizen studying at Harvard, set up an online photo management company, they thought hard about where to domicile Pixamo. Should they incorporate it in Ukraine, which has a simple and low tax structure but a problematic legal history? Or Switzerland, where taxes are higher but the legal system is well established? Or Delaware, where taxes are higher still but most U.S. start-ups are domiciled? Prihodko and Peyer eventually chose to base the company in the relatively tax-friendly Swiss canton of Zug, a decision that helped shareholders when they sold Pixamo to NameMedia in 2007.

Some global entrepreneurs must deal with several countries simultaneously, which is complex. In 1994, Gary Mueller launched Internet Securities to provide investors with data on emerging markets. Three years later, the start-up had offices in 18 countries and had to cope with the jurisdictions of Brazil, China, and Russia on any given day. By learning to do so, Internet Securities became a market leader, and in 1999, Euromoney acquired 80% of the company's equity for the tidy sum of $43 million.

Resources

Customers expect start-ups to possess the skills and deliver the levels of quality that larger companies do. That's a tall order for resource-stretched new ventures. Still, they have no option but to do whatever it takes to retain customers. In 1987, Jim Sharpe acquired a small business, XTech, now a manufacturer of faceplates for telecommunications equipment. Initially, the company made its products in the United States and sold them overseas through sales representatives and distributors. However, by 2006, Cisco, Lucent, Intel, IBM, and other XTech customers had shifted mostof their manufacturing to China. They became reluctant to do business with suppliers that didn't make products or have customer service operations in China. So Sharpe had no choice but to set up a subsidiary in China at that stage.

Competencies Global Entrepreneurs Need

All entrepreneurs must be able to identify opportunities, gather resources, and strike deals. They all must also possess soft skills like vision, leadership, and passion. To win globally, though, they must hone four additional competencies.

Articulating a Global Purpose

Developing a crystal clear rationale for being global is critical. In 1999, for example, Robert Wessman took

How Diaspora Networks Help Start-Ups Go Global

MANY ENTREPRENEURS HAVE TAKEN advantage of ethnic networks to formulate and execute a global strategy. The culture, values, and social norms members hold in common forge understanding and trust, making it easier to establish and enforce contracts.

Through diaspora networks, global entrepreneurs can quickly gain access to information, funding, talent, technology—and, of course, contacts. In the late 1990s, for instance, Boston-based Desh Deshpande, who had set up several high-tech ventures in the United States, was keen to start something in his native India. In April 2000, he met an optical communications expert, Kumar Sivarajan, who had worked at IBM's Watson Research Center before returning to India to take up a teaching position at the Indian Institute of Science in Bangalore. Deshpande introduced Sivarajan to two other Indians, Sanjay Nayak and Arnob Roy, who had both worked in the Indian subsidiaries of American high-tech companies. The trust among the four enabled the creation of the start-up Tejas Networks in two months' time. Deshpande and Sycamore Networks, the major investors, wired the initial capital of $5 million, attaching few of the usual conditions to the investment. Tejas Networks has become a leading telecommunications equipment manufacturer, generating revenues of around $100 million over the past year.

The research that my HBS colleague William Kerr and I have done suggests that entrepreneurs who most successfully exploit diaspora networks take these four steps:

---

control of a small pharmaceuticals maker in his native Iceland. Within weeks, he concluded that the generics player had to globalize its core functions—manufacturing, R&D, and marketing—to gain economies of scale, develop a large product portfolio, and be first to market with drugs as they came off patent. Since then, Actavis

Map Networks

The members of a diaspora often cluster in residential areas, public organizations, or industries. For instance, in Tokyo, Americans tend to work for professional service firms such as Morgan Stanley and McKinsey, live in Azabu, shop in Omotesand, and hang out at the American Club.

Identify Organizations That Can Help

Many countries have offices overseas that facilitate trade and investment, and they open their doors to people visiting from home. These organizations can provide the names of influential individuals, companies, and informal organizations, clubs, or groups.

Tap Informal Groups

Informal organizations of ethnic entrepreneurs and executives are usually located in communities where immigrant professionals are concentrated. In the United States, for instance, they thrive in high-tech industry neighborhoods such as Silicon Valley or universities like MIT.

Identify the Influentials

It can be tough to identify people who have standing with local businesses and also within the diaspora network. A board member or coach that both respect is an invaluable resource for a would-be entrepreneur.

---

has entered 40 countries, often by taking over local companies. Wessman faced numerous hurdles, but he stuck to the strategy. Actavis now makes 650 products and has 350 more in the pipeline. In 2007, it generated revenues of $2 billion and had become one of the world's top five generics manufacturers.

Alliance Building

Start-ups can quickly attain global reach by striking partnerships with large companies headquartered in other countries. However, most entrepreneurs have to enter into such deals from positions of weakness. An established company has managers who can conduct due diligence, the money to fly teams over for meetings, and the power to extract favorable terms from would-be partners. It has a reasonable period within which to negotiate a deal, and it has options in case talks with one company fail. A start-up has few of those resources or bargaining chips.

Start-ups also have problems communicating with global partners because their alliances have to span geographic and psychic distances. Take the case of Trolltech, an open-source software company founded in 1994 in Oslo by Eirik Chambe-Eng and Haavard Nord. In 2001, the start-up landed a contract to supply a Japanese manufacturer with a Linux-based software platform for personal digital assistants (PDAs). The dream order quickly turned into a nightmare. There were differences between what the Japanese company thought it would get and what the Norwegian supplier felt it should provide, and the start-up struggled to deliver the modifications its partner began to demand. Suspecting that Trolltech wouldn't deliver the software on time, the Japanese company offered to send over a team of software engineers. However, when it suggested that both companies work through the Christmas break to meet a deadline—a common practice in Japan—Trolltech refused, citing the importance of the Christmas vacation in Norway. The relationship almost collapsed, but Chambe-Eng and Nord managed to negotiate a new deadline that they could meet without having to work during the holiday season.

Supply-Chain Creation

Entrepreneurs must often choose suppliers on the other side of the world and monitor them without having managers nearby. Besides, the best manufacturing locations change as labor and fuel costs rise and as quality problems show up, as they did in China.

Start-ups find it daunting to manage complex supply networks, but they gain competitive advantage by doing so. Sometimes the global supply chain lies at the heart of the business opportunity. Take the case of Winery Exchange, cofounded by Peter Byck in 1999. The California-based venture manages a 22-country network of wineries and breweries. Winery Exchange works closely with retail chains, such as Kroger, Tesco, and Costco, to develop premium private label products, and it gets its suppliers to produce and package the wines as inexpensively as possible. The venture has succeeded because it links relatively small market-needy suppliers with mammoth product-hungry retailers and provides both with its product development expertise. In 2006, Winery Exchange sold 2 million cases of 330 different brands of wine, beer, and spirits to retailers on four continents.

In addition to raw materials and components, start-ups are increasingly buying intellectual property from across the world. Hands-On Mobile, started by David

How Social Entrepreneurs
Think Global

ATSUMASA TOCHISAKO IS AN unlikely entrepreneur. When he was in his mid-fifties, he left a senior position at the Bank of Tokyo-Mitsubishi to set up Microfinance International, a global for-profit social enterprise (FOPSE, for short), based in Washington, D.C. Having also been stationed in Latin America for many years, Tochisako had observed the large cash remittances coming from immigrants in the United States, as well as the exorbitant charges they paid commercial banks and the poor service they received. Sensing a business opportunity and the chance to do some good, he decided to provide immigrant workers with inexpensive remittance, check-cashing, insurance, and microlending services.

MFI was international from its birth in June 2003, with operations in the United States and El Salvador. Since then, it has expanded into a dozen Latin American countries and further extended its reach by allowing multinational financial institutions, such as the UAE Exchange, to use its proprietary Internet-based settlement platform.

Kranzler, is a Silicon Valley–based developer of the mobile versions of Guitar Hero III, Iron Man, and other games. When the company started in 2001, the markets for mobile multimedia content were developing faster in Asia and Europe than in the United States, and gamers were creating attractive products in China, South Korea, and Japan. Kranzler realized that his company had to acquire intellectual property and design capacity overseas in order to offer customers a comprehensive catalog of games and the latest delivery technologies. Hands-On

Like Tochisako, many entrepreneurs today combine social values, profit motive, and a global focus. Social entrepreneurs are global from birth for three reasons. First, disease, malnutrition, poverty, illiteracy, and other social problems exist on a large scale in many developing countries. Second, the resources—funds, institutions, and governance systems—to tackle those issues are mainly in the developed world. Third, FOPSEs that tackle specific conditions can often be adapted to other countries. For instance, in 2002, Shane Immelman founded The Lapdesk Company to provide portable desks to South African schoolchildren, a third of whom are taught in schoolrooms that don't have adequate surfaces on which to write. The company asks large corporations in South Africa to donate desks—with some advertising on them—for entire school districts. By doing so, these companies are able to meet the South African government's requirement that they invest part of their profits in black empowerment programs. Since then, Immelman has adapted the business model to Kenya, Nigeria, and the Democratic Republic of Congo and has launched programs in India and Latin America.

Mobile therefore picked up MobileGame Korea, as well as two Chinese content development companies, which has helped it become a market leader.

Multinational Organization

In 2006, I conducted a simulation exercise called the Virtual Entrepreneurial Team Exercise (VETE) for 450 MBA students in 10 business schools in Argentina, Austria, Brazil, England, Hong Kong, Liechtenstein, the Netherlands, Japan, and the United States. The teams, each composed of students from different schools and different countries, developed hypothetical pitches for Asia Renal Care, a Hong Kong–based medical services start-up, that had raised its first round of capital in 1999. They experienced a slice of global entrepreneurial life in real time, using technologies like Skype, wikis, virtual chat rooms, and, of course, e-mail to communicate with one another. The students learned how to build trust, compensate for the lack of visual cues, respect cultural differences, and deal with different institutional frameworks and incentives—the competencies entrepreneurs need for coordination, control, and communication in global enterprises. The would-be entrepreneurs' emotions ranged from elation to frustration, and their output varied from good to excellent.

Start-ups cope with the challenges of managing a global organization in different ways. Internet Securities used a knowledge database to share information among its offices around the world, increasing managers' ability to recognize and solve problems. RacingThePlanet used intensive training to ensure that volunteers perform at a consistently high level during the events it holds. Trolltech worked round the clock to meet deadlines, passing off development tasks from teams in Norway to those in Australia as the day ends in one place and begins in the other. Inverness Medical hired key executives wherever it could and organized the company around them rather than move people all over the world.

Still, there are no easy answers to the challenges of managing a start-up in the topsy-turvy world of global entrepreneurship. Take the case of Mei Zhang, who founded WildChina, a high-end adventure-tourism company in China, in 2000. Three years later, Zhang hired an American expatriate, Jim Stent, who had a deep interest in Chinese history and culture, as her COO. Zhang moved to Los Angeles in 2004, anointing Stent as CEO in Beijing and appointing herself chairperson. Thus, a Chinese expatriate living in the United States had to supervise an American expatriate living in Beijing. And when the two amicably parted ways in 2006, Zhang started managing the Chinese company from Los Angeles. These are contingencies no textbook provides for.

Entrepreneurs shouldn't fear the fact that the world isn't flat. Being global may not be a pursuit for the fainthearted, but even start-ups can thrive by using distance to gain competitive advantage.

DANIEL J. ISENBERG is a senior lecturer at Harvard Business School.

Originally published in December 2008. Reprint R0812J.

Giving Up the CEO Seat

by Jeffrey Hollender

IT HAPPENED THREE YEARS ago, but my memory of the moment I knew I had to step down as CEO is indelible. On the morning after a long business trip to the West Coast, I was returning to the Burlington, Vermont, headquarters of the company I had cofounded, Seventh Generation. As I walked through our offices, with their view of Lake Champlain and the Adirondacks' distant peaks, I resumed my daily ritual of seeking out associates with whom I didn't regularly connect. But this time I was struck by a startling realization: People were clicking away at their computers, huddling in conference rooms, or heading out for meetings—*and I had no idea what they were working on*. The experience unnerved me.

As the chief executive, I had long been intimately involved in many of Seventh Generation's inner workings. My team often found my preoccupation with the details both impressive and annoying. I would constantly bird-dog efforts to make our diapers absorb just one more gram of liquid. I'd focus relentlessly on new styles of perforation for our toilet tissue. I worked with our sales director on setting goals for every item we sold, right down to individual distribution channels and accounts. In meetings I took meticulous notes on each direct report, listing every commitment and project deadline. But something had changed.

Even as I shook off the jet lag, this new, discomfiting feeling of detachment persisted. Even worse, it escalated. I found myself baffled by two of Seventh Generation's most challenging strategic decisions: whether to sell our household and personal-care products at Wal-Mart, and whether to expand the brand outside the United States. For the first time in my career, I was at a loss for answers or ideas.

Intellectually, I was in denial. But in my gut, I felt ill prepared to take Seventh Generation—which in 2007 generated $93 million in annual sales—to its then stated goal of $250 million. Having steered the company for nearly two decades, I knew it was time to find a new CEO.

A Difficult Transition

Any senior leadership transition is fraught with challenges, none more so than when a company founder abdicates the top job. Each morning, as I sat in silence after my hour of predawn exercise, I'd reflect on executives who had bungled their transitions. Two glaring examples were from high tech: Michael Dell left too early, and Scott McNealy left too late. When Dell handed the reins of his namesake company to a trusted lieutenant,

Idea of Brief

The CEO and cofounder of Seventh Generation, a maker of environmentally responsible household and personal care products, describes how he came to realize that although he'd been the right person to guide his company through its infancy and adolescence, he was not the right one to take it into full-fledged adulthood. Having made the decision to step down, he had to determine the best way to proceed: How quickly should he move? How public should he be? How would he get buy-in from the board and the company's associates? How would he ensure that Seventh Generation's fierce commitment to social and environmental sustainability endured? Most important, was he doing the right thing?

it was the world's largest PC maker; within three years rivals had clawed away much of Dell's market share, and its founder was compelled to return as CEO. Conversely, McNealy continued as chief of Sun Microsystems despite the company's stunted growth and falling share price. By the time he stepped down, Sun's eventual sale to Oracle was almost inevitable. But then there's Oprah Winfrey, who announced at the peak of her success that she would leave her iconic show in 2011, causing David Carr to write in the *New York Times* that her "gut intuition, about knowing when to say no and when it is time to go, is worth studying at every business graduate school in the country."

The tangible costs of a bungled transition can run to hundreds of millions of dollars' worth of squandered market share and submerged sales. But I was more concerned with avoiding damage to Seventh Generation's intangible assets: our associates' spirit and will, our stakeholders' trust, and our company's mission and reputation.

Seventh Generation aspires to do more than simply grow market share. Its purpose is to inspire a more conscious and sustainable world by being an authentic force for positive change. Profits are the score, not the game. But to fulfill the company's mission, we had to become bigger and more profitable. We needed a CEO who would use our financial imperatives to fuel our social and environmental imperatives—someone few executive recruiters are equipped to find. Not surprisingly, the more I thought about how best to proceed, the more questions arose: How quickly should I move? How public should I be? How would I get the board's support and associates' buy-in? How would I ensure that Seventh Generation's fierce commitment to social and environmental sustainability endured? Above all, was I doing the right thing? (Every family member and close colleague said no.)

Seventh Generation's directors wondered if they were about to lose the best investment in their portfolios: In 2007 alone, I had helped grow the business by more than 40%. Some staffers thought that no one who replaced me would have the same vision and values. Talented people signed on with Seventh Generation precisely because it explicitly promised to be a place where they could summon all their individuality and creativity—the very attributes that many companies insist be left at home. Associates worried that a new CEO would fill the place with corporate drones. My wife fretted that I'd end up at home, bored and depressed.

Nevertheless, we found a way to welcome the biggest change in the company's history. Last June, Seventh

Generation got a new chief, Chuck Maniscalco, who until 2008 had been president and CEO of PepsiCo's nearly $10 billion Quaker, Tropicana, and Gatorade division. I remain at the company as executive chairman (Chuck reports to the board, not to me), and I've been devoting much of my energy to furthering Seventh Generation's mission, vision, and corporate-responsibility strategy. No one can predict the future, but early returns confirm that making the transition was the right thing to do.

Transition Tenets

It was tough to concede that I was the best person to guide our company through infancy and adolescence but not into full-fledged adulthood. I overcame lots of obstacles by following several transition principles involving community, transparency, mission, and corporate consciousness—all central to building a purpose-driven organization. As I learned through real-world experience, they're also valuable signposts for finding a new CEO.

Look Unflinchingly at Your Own Performance
For the better part of the past decade, Seventh Generation (with help from the author and consultant Carol Sanford) has been trying to develop its corporate consciousness—to make us more sharply aware of how we work and what we want to accomplish. Sure, the phrase exudes a whiff of the mystical (or at least the mysterious). But the idea is inherently tough-minded: Break ingrained habits of thought, kick over stale ideas, and avoid the easy path of simply repeating past successes.

In late 2007, when I first seriously considered recruiting a replacement, Seventh Generation was enjoying the best run in its history. In 2008 our sales approached $140 million, an unprecedented 51% jump over the previous year's record sales. To some it seemed the height of folly to bring in a new chief when the company was performing at its peak. Reed Doyle, a passionate, committed member of our product development team, summed up a lot of people's misgivings when he rose at one of our town hall–style meetings and let me have it. "How do we know," he inquired, "that you won't screw up our success by bringing in some corporate big shot?"

Actually, I worried that our success was vulnerable to other threats. Although we sometimes seemed to be moving with relative ease down well-worn roads, we were heading into new territory, populated by bigger, fiercer rivals. The company had historically been only marginally profitable, our significant growth masking our meager earnings; that was no longer acceptable for a company of our size. To compete with the giants of the consumer packaged goods (CPG) industry, we'd have to grow annual sales from $140 million to $500 million and eventually $1 billion, and earn double-digit operating profits.

As objectively as I could, I assessed my ability to lead Seventh Generation toward billion-dollar growth. Our ERP and other software systems had failed to keep pace with the company's expansion. My lack of interest in logistics was partly to blame for our inability to cut transportation and warehousing costs in half. And my senior managers would describe me as the CEO who never met an investment he didn't like: I saw only the upside, never wanting to dwell on the consequences of investments gone wrong.

When I was ruthlessly honest with myself, I couldn't help concluding that my limitations bled the benefits of my staying on as CEO. And I lacked the fire. Only when I began to think about taking on a greater cause, such as helping other companies weave sustainability into all their operations, did my pulse begin to quicken.

In the spirit of raising corporate consciousness—and to persuade the company's directors—I wrote the business case for my succession and presented it to the board. First, I outlined my greatest value to the company moving forward: to be out in public, increasing Seventh Generation's brand awareness and advancing our mission of creating a better world for future generations. Next, I argued that my lack of experience running a far bigger company reduced my effectiveness as a leader. Finally, I asserted that we needed a chief executive who knew how to build out a consumer brand while competing with huge CPG companies.

My presentation was met with stunned silence. I had shared my plans with a few board members ahead of time, but even they were at a loss as to how to respond to my passionate plea. Then, after a few polite questions—How quickly did I expect this transition to happen? What if we couldn't find the right person? How did I think the staff would respond?—the board found its equilibrium and agreed conceptually (though not wholeheartedly) that bringing in a new leader was the right decision. Its members wouldn't commit to a transition, however, until they were confident that we'd

---

Steady growth at Seventh Generation

How sales fared under Jeffrey Hollender

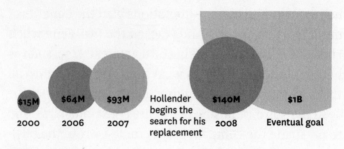

| $15M | $64M | $93M | Hollender begins the search for his replacement | $140M | $1B |
| 2000 | 2006 | 2007 | | 2008 | Eventual goal |

Source: Seventh Generation

---

found the right successor. I thought that recruiting a seasoned number-two executive—a president who would oversee the company's operations but report to me instead of the board, and would become CEO in one to three years—would make for a smooth transition. But reality has a way of disrupting even the best-laid plans.

Dare To Be Transparent

Not long ago the founder and CEO of another values-driven company covertly recruited a successor, declining to go public until the day the new chief arrived. The sudden, unexpected change lowered associates' morale and productivity and made the new leader's job even more challenging. Secrecy is counterproductive, whereas transparency calms the chatter that so often accompanies significant change.

At one of our monthly all-hands meetings, I made the case to the entire Seventh Generation community for why I should step aside. At first people were skeptical, somewhat scared, and hungry for details. "How would we know that a new chief shared our values?" someone asked. "How do we know the new leader won't come in and flip the business for a quick profit?" someone else said. "Will we have a voice in the selection process—and how quickly is this going to happen?"

Our associates own close to 20% of the company; thus, I argued, what was best for the business was best for them. More than a few no doubt remained apprehensive about the changes to come—as I did. But I updated the staff on the search every four to six weeks and convened a team of senior and junior associates to meet with every serious candidate. Getting more minds into the mix would help us make a better decision, and we all felt that if the process remained open and transparent, we'd arrive at a good outcome.

Make the Company's Mission Central in Your Search

Seventh Generation is organized around seven "global imperatives"—three of which are that we work to restore the environment, help create a just and equitable world, and encourage associates to think of themselves as educators dedicated to inspiring conscious consumption. If these goals sound impossibly utopian, that is part of the intent. Defining ourselves as evangelists for social and environmental sustainability sets the company apart.

Before we began interviewing, I created a spreadsheet to rate candidates on qualities in three categories: essential, important, and nice to have. (See the sidebar

Screening the Field

BEFORE WE BEGAN INTERVIEWING candidates, I created a spreadsheet of certain qualities I was looking for in my replacement. I divided them into three categories: essential, important, and nice to have.

Essential

Committed to the mission

Good chemistry with the company's values

Experience growing an organization

Demonstrated strategic-planning abilities

Vision

The capacity for self-reflection

Self-motivation

Leadership capabilities

Lack of ego

Important

Commitment to corporate social responsibility

A clear understanding of Seventh Generation's markets and goals

Nice to have

High level of curiosity

Openness to different business models and ideas

"Screening the Field.") Most essential was a commitment to fulfilling our mission of deeper business purpose—without which no one would make the first cut. Other must-haves included high-growth management experience, demonstrated strategic ability, and leadership capability.

Some might argue against my putting "values" at the top of the list—especially when we were heading into the teeth of a global recession. But I had already seen, in the course of recruiting executives to our senior management team, how our values helped us punch far above our weight class. Ambitious veterans who'd made their mark at heavyweights like Clorox, P&G, and Quaker Oats sought us out precisely because they wanted their work to make a positive difference in the world.

Chuck Maniscalco is proof of that. Just two weeks after he took over as CEO, he blogged that he had joined Seventh Generation because he was drawn to the company's mission. "I am at a point in my life of wanting, almost desperately, to give back," he wrote. But lest anyone think he's a softie, consider this: Out of the 70 candidates we reviewed, Chuck was the only one who wasn't interested in a number-two job. He made a persuasive case that to take the company where it needed to go, he would have to be the chief executive. I would have to immediately turn over the CEO post and redefine my role at the company. Considering all that Chuck had accomplished, and all that he could do for Seventh Generation, I knew I couldn't refuse.

The week before Chuck was scheduled to revisit Burlington for a final round of meetings, I convened with my senior managers and put three questions to each: Should Chuck be CEO or president? How quickly should we make the transition? What operational responsibilities should I retain for the first six months of his tenure? I thought they would ask me to stay at the top for as long as possible. I was wrong. With only one exception, each declared that it was time for me to move on—the sooner, the better. In their view, the transition was already under way.

As I reflected on their recommendation during my drive home, I was both saddened and angered. Part of me felt they'd been deeply disloyal. But at the same time, I knew they were doing what I always demanded—speaking the truth without political considerations. By the end of my half-hour commute, I knew that this 20-year chapter of my life was nearing its conclusion. I had to get ready to let go.

I'm now deeply involved in building initiatives to ensure that progressive businesses have more influence in shaping public policy. The most exciting of these is the American Sustainable Business Council, a challenger to the U.S. Chamber of Commerce. Chuck is fully engaged in running Seventh Generation. Time will ultimately tell whether we made the right moves. (I believe we did.) But I have no doubt that by using the transition principles above, we followed the right path.

Note

Jeffrey Hollender wrote this article with Bill Breen *(bbreen@billbreen.net), Seventh Generation's editorial director and a former senior projects editor at* Fast Company. *They are the coauthors of* The Responsibility Revolution: How the Next Generation of Businesses Will Win *(Jossey-Bass, 2010). Portions of this article have been adapted from the book.*

JEFFREY HOLLENDER is a cofounder and the executive chairman of Seventh Generation, a maker of environmentally responsible products.

Originally published in March 2010. Reprint R1003J

The Founder's Dilemma

by Noam Wasserman

EVERY WOULD-BE ENTREPRENEUR wants to be a Bill Gates, a Phil Knight, or an Anita Roddick, each of whom founded a large company and led it for many years. However, successful CEO-cum-founders are a very rare breed. When I analyzed 212 American start-ups that sprang up in the late 1990s and early 2000s, I discovered that most founders surrendered management control long before their companies went public. By the time the ventures were three years old, 50% of founders were no longer the CEO; in year four, only 40% were still in the corner office; and fewer than 25% led their companies' initial public offerings. Other researchers have subsequently found similar trends in various industries and in other time periods. We remember the handful of founder-CEOs in corporate America, but they're the exceptions to the rule.

Founders don't let go easily, though. Four out of five entrepreneurs, my research shows, are forced to step down from the CEO's post. Most are shocked when investors insist that they relinquish control, and they're pushed out of office in ways they don't like and well before they want to abdicate. The change in leadership can be particularly damaging when employees loyal to the founder oppose it. In fact, the manner in which founders tackle their first leadership transition often makes or breaks young enterprises.

The transitions take place relatively smoothly if, at the outset, founders are honest about their motives for getting into business. Isn't that obvious, you may ask. Don't people start a business to make pots of money? They do. However, a 2000 paper in the *Journal of Political Economy* and another two years later in the *American Economic Review* showed that entrepreneurs as a class make only as much money as they could have if they had been employees. In fact, entrepreneurs make less, if you account for the higher risk. What's more, in my experience, founders often make decisions that conflict with the wealth-maximization principle. As I studied the choices before entrepreneurs, I noticed that some options had the potential for generating higher financial gains but others, which founders often chose, conflicted with the desire for money.

The reason isn't hard to fathom: There is, of course, another factor motivating entrepreneurs along with the desire to become wealthy: the drive to create and lead an organization. The surprising thing is that trying to maximize one imperils achievement of the other. Entrepreneurs face a choice, at every step, between making money and managing their ventures. Those who don't

Idea in Brief

Most entrepreneurs want to make pots of money *and* run the show. But Wasserman reveals that it's tough to do both. If you don't figure out which matters most to you, you could end up being neither rich nor in control.

Consider: To make a lot of money from a new venture, you need financial resources to capitalize on the opportunities before you. That means attracting investors—which requires relinquishing control as you give away equity and as investors alter your board's membership. To remain in charge of your business, you have to keep more equity. But that means fewer financial resources to fuel your venture.

So, you must choose between money and power. Begin by articulating your primary motivation for starting a business. Then understand the trade-offs associated with that goal. As your venture unfolds, you'll make choices that support—rather than jeopardize—your dreams.

figure out which is more important to them often end up neither wealthy nor powerful.

Inside the Founder's Mind

Founders are usually convinced that only they can lead their start-ups to success. "I'm the one with the vision and the desire to build a great company. I have to be the one running it," several entrepreneurs have told me. There's a great deal of truth to that view. At the start, the enterprise is only an idea in the mind of its founder, who possesses all the insights about the opportunity; about the innovative product, service, or business model that will capitalize on that opportunity; and about who the potential customers are. The founder hires people to build the business according to that vision and develops close relationships with those

Idea in Practice

At every step in their venture's life, entrepreneurs face a choice between making money and controlling their businesses. And each choice comes with a trade-off.

If You Want to Get Rich

Startup founders who give up more equity to attract cofounders, key executives, and investors build more valuable companies than those who part with less equity. And the founder ends up with a more valuable slice of the pie.

On the other hand, to attract investors and executives, you have to cede control of most decision making. And once you're no longer in control, your job as CEO is at risk. That's because:

- You need broader skills—such as creating formal processes and developing specialized roles—to continue building your company than you did to start it. This stretches most founders' abilities beyond their limits, and investors may force you to step down.

- Investors dole out money in stages. At each stage, they add their own people to your board, gradually threatening your control.

If you're motivated more by wealth than power:

- Recognize when the top job has stretched beyond your

first employees. The founder creates the organizational culture, which is an extension of his or her style, personality, and preferences. From the get-go, employees, customers, and business partners identify start-ups with their founders, who take great pride in their founder-cum-CEO status.

New ventures are usually labors of love for entrepreneurs, and they become emotionally attached to them, referring to the business as "my baby" and using similar parenting language without even noticing. Their attachment is evident in the relatively low salaries they capabilities, and hire a new CEO yourself.

- Work with your board to develop post-succession roles for yourself.

- Be open to pursuing ideas that require external financing.

If You Want to Run the Company

To retain control of your new business, you may need to bootstrap the venture— using your own capital instead of taking money from investors. You'll have less financial fuel to increase your company's value. But you'll be able to continue running the company yourself.

If you're more motivated by power than wealth:

- Restrict yourself to businesses where you already have the skills and contacts you need.

- Focus on a business in which large amounts of capital aren't required to get your venture off the ground and flying.

- Consider waiting until late in your career before setting up shop for a new venture. That will give you time to develop the broader skills you'll need as your business grows and to accumulate some savings for bootstrapping.

pay themselves. My study of compensation in 528 new ventures set up between 1996 and 2002 showed that 51% of entrepreneurs made the same money as—or made less than—at least one person who reported to them. Even though they had comparable backgrounds, they received 20% less in cash compensation than non-founders who performed similar roles. That was so even after taking into account the value of the equity each person held.

Many entrepreneurs are overconfident about their prospects and naive about the problems they will face.

For instance, in 1988, Purdue University strategy scholar Arnold Cooper and two colleagues asked 3,000 entrepreneurs two simple questions: "What are the odds of your business succeeding?" and "What are the odds of any business like yours succeeding?" Founders claimed that there was an 81% chance, on average, that they would succeed but only a 59% probability of success for other ventures like their own. In fact, 80% of the respondents pegged their chances of success at at least 70%—and one in three claimed their likelihood of success was 100%. Founders' attachment, overconfidence, and naïveté may be necessary to get new ventures up and running, but these emotions later create problems.

Growing Pains

Founders eventually realize that their financial resources, ability to inspire people, and passion aren't enough to enable their ventures to capitalize fully on the opportunities before them. They invite family members and friends, angel investors, or venture capital firms to invest in their companies. In doing so, they pay a heavy price: They often have to give up total control over the enterprise. Angel investors may allow entrepreneurs to retain control to a greater degree than venture capital firms do, but in both cases, outside directors will join the company's board.

Once the founder is no longer in control of the board, his or her job as CEO is at risk. The board's task is straight-forward if the founder underperforms as CEO, although even when founders are floundering, boards can have a hard time persuading them to put their "babies" up for adoption. But, paradoxically, the need for a change at the top becomes even greater when a founder has delivered results. Let me explain why.

The first major task in any new venture is the development of its product or service. Many founders believe that if they've successfully led the development of the organization's first new offering, that's ample proof of their management prowess. They think investors should have no cause for complaint and should continue to back their leadership. "Since I've gotten us to the stage where the product is ready, that should tell them that I can lead this company" is a common refrain.

Their success makes it harder for founders to realize that when they celebrate the shipping of the first products, they're marking the end of an era. At that point, leaders face a different set of business challenges. The founder has to build a company capable of marketing and selling large volumes of the product and of providing customers with after-sales service. The venture's finances become more complex, and the CEO needs to depend on finance executives and accountants. The organization has to become more structured, and the CEO has to create formal processes, develop specialized roles, and, yes, institute a managerial hierarchy. The dramatic broadening of the skills that the CEO needs at this stage stretches most founders' abilities beyond their limits.

A technology-oriented founder-CEO, for instance, may be the best person to lead a start-up during its early days, but as the company grows, it will need someone with different skills. Indeed, in analyzing the boards of 450 privately held ventures, I found that outside investors control the board more often where the CEO is a founder, where the CEO has a background in science or technology rather than in marketing or sales, and where the CEO has on average 13 years of experience.

Thus, the faster that founder-CEOs lead their companies to the point where they need outside funds and new management skills, the quicker they will lose management control. Success makes founders less qualified to lead the company and changes the power structure so they are more vulnerable. "Congrats, you're a success! Sorry, you're fired," is the implicit message that many investors have to send founder-CEOs.

Investors wield the most influence over entrepreneurs just before they invest in their companies, often using that moment to force founders to step down. A recent report in *Private Equity Week* pithily captures this dynamic: "Seven Networks Inc., a Redwood City, Calif.-based mobile email company, has raised $42 million in new venture capital funding. . . . In other Seven news, the company named former Onebox.com CEO Russ Bott as its new CEO."

The founder's moment of truth sometimes comes quickly. One Silicon Valley–based venture capital firm, for instance, insists on owning at least 50% of any start-up after the first round of financing. Other investors, to reduce their risk, dole money out in stages, and each round alters the board's composition, gradually threatening the entrepreneur's control over the company. Then it usually takes two or three rounds of financing

The trade-off entrepreneurs make

Founders' choices are straightforward: Do they want to be rich or king? Few have been both.

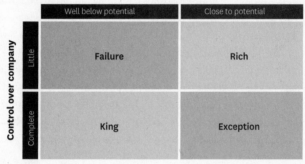

before outsiders acquire more than 50% of a venture's equity. In such cases, investors allow founder-CEOs to lead their enterprises longer, since the founder will have to come back for more capital, but at some point outsiders will gain control of the board.

Whether gradual or sudden, the transition is often stormy. In 2001, for instance, when a California-based internet telephony company finished developing the first generation of its system, an outside investor pushed for the appointment of a new CEO. He felt the company needed an executive experienced at managing the other executives who oversaw the firm's existing functions, had deeper knowledge of the functions the venture would have to create, and had experience in instituting

Keeping Founders on Board

WHAT DO BOARDS DO with founders after asking them to step down as CEO? Ideally, a board should keep the founder involved in some way, often as a board member, and use his or her relationships and knowledge to help the new CEO succeed. As one investor stated, "You can replace an executive, but you can't replace a founder."

Many times, keeping the founder on board is easier said than done. Founders can act, sometimes unconsciously, as negative forces. They can resist the changes suggested by new CEOs and encourage their loyalists to leave. Some boards and CEOs try to manage those risks by taking half-measures, relegating the founder to a cosmetic role, but that can backfire. For instance, at Wily Technology, Lew Cirne agreed to become chief technology officer after giving up the CEO's post; later he saw that not a single person reported to him. His successor also wanted Cirne to give up his position as board chairman. These moves increased Cirne's unhappiness.

In my study of succession in technology start-ups, I found that 37% of founder-CEOs left their companies when a professional CEO came in, 23% took a position below the CEO, and 40% moved into the chairman's role. Another study of high-growth firms reported that, of the founder-CEOs who were replaced, around 25% left their companies while 50% remained on the board of directors for the next five years.

---

new processes to knit together the company's activities. The founder refused to accept the need for a change, and it took five pressure-filled months of persuasion before he would step down.

He's not the only one to have fought the inevitable; four out of five founder-CEOs I studied resisted the idea, too. If the need for change is clear to the board, why isn't it clear to the founder? Because the founder's emotional strengths become liabilities at this stage.

Boards can sometimes help founders find new roles. When a founder has an affinity for a particular functional area, such as engineering, the board can offer him or her the luxury of focusing on that area and letting the new CEO "take on all the things you don't like to do." That approach helps founders gain an appreciation for the new CEO's abilities. The more concrete value the new CEO adds, the easier it will be for the founder to accept the transition. What's more, the less similar the new CEO is to the founder—if the new CEO is 10 years older, for instance—the easier it is for the founder to accept the change.

Founders who want to be CEO for a longer time in their next venture need to learn new skills. Accordingly, boards can encourage founders to take on new roles in their companies that will enable them to do so. If they do, founders may even become accomplished enough to regain control. For example, in 1998, when E Ink's board appointed a new CEO, cofounder Russ Wilcox identified skills he needed to strengthen. He therefore rotated through roles in finance, product marketing, sales, and even R&D to fill the gaps in his skill set. In 2004, when the board launched a search for the company's next CEO, it couldn't find anyone more qualified for the job than Wilcox himself and made him CEO—a position he has held ever since.

Used to being the heart and soul of their ventures, founders find it hard to accept lesser roles, and their resistance triggers traumatic leadership transitions within young companies.

Time to Choose

As start-ups grow, entrepreneurs face a dilemma—one that many aren't aware of, initially. On the one hand, they have to raise resources in order to capitalize on the opportunities before them. If they choose the right investors, their financial gains will soar. My research shows that a founder who gives up more equity to attract cofounders, nonfounding hires, and investors builds a more valuable company than one who parts with less equity. The founder ends up with a more valuable slice, too. On the other hand, in order to attract investors and executives, entrepreneurs have to give up control over most decision making.

This fundamental tension yields "rich" versus "king" trade-offs. The "rich" options enable the company to become more valuable but sideline the founder by taking away the CEO position and control over major decisions. The "king" choices allow the founder to retain control of decision making by staying CEO and maintaining control over the board—but often only by building a less valuable company. For founders, a "rich" choice isn't necessarily better than a "king" choice, or vice versa; what matters is how well each decision fits with their reason for starting the company.

Consider, for example, Ockham Technologies' cofounder and CEO Jim Triandiflou, who realized in 2000 that he would have to attract investors to stay in business. Soon, he had several suitors wooing him, including an inexperienced angel investor and a well-known venture capital firm. The angel investor's offer would have left Triandiflou in control of the board: Joining him on it would be only his cofounder and the angel investor himself. If he accepted the other offer, though, he would control just two of five seats on the board.

Triandiflou felt that Ockham would grow bigger if he roped in the venture capital firm rather than the angel investor. After much soul-searching, he decided to take a risk, and he sold an equity stake to the venture firm. He gave up board control, but in return he gained resources and expertise that helped increase Ockham's value manifold.

Similarly, at Wily Technology, a Silicon Valley enterprise software company, founder Lew Cirne gave up control of the board and the company in exchange for financial backing from Greylock Partners and other venture capital firms. As a result, CA bought Wily two years later for far more money than it would have if Cirne had tried to go it alone.

On the other side of the coin are founders who bootstrap their ventures in order to remain in control. For instance, John Gabbert, the founder of Room & Board, is a successful Minneapolis-based furniture retailer. Having set up nine stores, he has repeatedly rejected offers of funding that would enable the company to grow faster, fearing that would lead him to lose control. As he told *BusinessWeek* in October 2007, "The trade-offs are just too great." Gabbert is clearly willing to live with the choices he has made as long as he can run the company himself.

Most founder-CEOs start out by wanting both wealth and power. However, once they grasp that they'll probably have to maximize one or the other, they will be in a position to figure out which is more important to them. Their past decisions regarding cofounders, hires, and investors will usually tell them which they truly favor. Once they know, they will find it easier to tackle transitions.

Founders who understand that they are motivated more by wealth than by control will themselves bring in new CEOs. For example, at one health care–focused internet venture based in California, the founder-CEO held a series of discussions with potential investors, which helped him uncover his own motivations. He eventually told the investors that he wanted to "do as well as I can from an equity perspective. . . [and do] what will be required for the company to be successful in the long run." Once he had articulated that goal, he started playing an active role in the search for a new CEO. Such founders are also likely to work with their boards to develop post-succession roles for themselves.

By contrast, founders who understand that they are motivated by control are more prone to making decisions that enable them to lead the business at the expense of increasing its value. They are more likely to remain sole founders, to use their own capital instead of taking money from investors, to resist deals that affect their management control, and to attract executives who will not threaten their desire to run the company. For instance, in 2002, the founder-CEO of a Boston-based information technology venture wanted to raise $5 million in a first round of financing. During negotiations with potential investors, he realized that all of them would insist on bringing in a professional CEO. Saying that he "was not going to hand the company over to someone else," the entrepreneur decided to raise only $2 million, and he remained CEO for the next two years.

One factor affecting the founder's choices is the perception of a venture's potential. Founders often make different decisions when they believe their start-ups have the potential to grow into extremely valuable companies than when they believe their ventures won't be that valuable. For instance, serial entrepreneur Evan Williams built Pyra Labs, the company that coined the term "blogger" and started the Blogger.com site, without the help of outside investors and eventually sold it to Google in 2003. By contrast, two years later, for his next venture, the podcasting company Odeo, Williams quickly brought in Charles River Ventures to invest $4 million. Asked why, Williams told the *Wall Street Journal* in October 2005: "We thought we had the opportunity to do something more substantial [with Odeo]." Having ceded control quickly in an effort to realize the substantial potential of the company, Williams has had a change of heart, buying back the company in 2006 and regaining his kingship.

Some venture capitalists implicitly use the trade-off between money and control to judge whether they should invest in founder-led companies. A few take it to the extreme by refusing to back founders who aren't motivated by money. Others invest in a start-up only when they're confident the founder has the skills to lead it in the long term. Even these firms, though, have to replace as many as a quarter of the founder-CEOs in the companies they fund.

Rich-or-king choices can also crop up in established companies. One of my favorite examples comes from history. In 1917, Henry Royce was pushed to merge

Rolls-Royce with Vickers, a large armaments manufacturer, in order to form a stronger British company. In a chapter in *Creating Modern Capitalism*, Peter Botticelli records Royce's reaction: "From a personal point of view, I prefer to be absolute boss over my own department (even if it was extremely small) rather than to be associated with a much larger technical department over which I had only joint control." Royce wanted control—not money.

Heads of not-for-profit organizations must make similar choices. I recently consulted with a successful Virginia-based nonprofit whose founder-CEO had faced two coup attempts. Early on, a hospital executive who felt he was himself more qualified to lead the organization mounted one takeover bid, and some years later, a board member made the other bid when the venture was beginning to attract notice. The founder realized that if he continued to accept money from outside organizations, he would face more attempts to oust him. Now the question he and his family have to think through is whether to take less money from outside funders even though that means the venture will grow less quickly.

Would-be entrepreneurs can also apply the framework to judge the kind of ideas they should pursue. Those desiring control should restrict themselves to businesses where they already have the skills and contacts they need or where large amounts of capital aren't required. They may also want to wait until late in their careers before setting up shop, after they have developed broader skills and accumulated some savings.

Founders who want to become wealthy should be open to pursuing ideas that require resources. They can make the leap sooner because they won't mind taking money from investors or depending on executives to manage their ventures.

Choosing between money and power allows entrepreneurs to come to grips with what success means to them. Founders who want to manage empires will not believe they are successes if they lose control, even if they end up rich. Conversely, founders who understand that their goal is to amass wealth will not view themselves as failures when they step down from the top job. Once they realize why they are turning entrepreneur, founders must, as the old Chinese proverb says, "decide on three things at the start: the rules of the game, the stakes, and the quitting time."

NOAM WASSERMAN is an associate professor at Harvard Business School.

Originally published in February 2008. Reprint R0802G

Why Entrepreneurs Don't Scale

by John Hamm

IT'S A CLICHÉ TO SAY that founders flounder, but unfortunately, that's usually the case. Wild exceptions like Bill Gates, Steve Jobs, and Michael Dell aside, executives who start a business or project fizzle more often than not once they've gotten their venture on its feet.

Entrepreneurs actually show their inability to switch to executive mode much earlier in the business development process than most people realize, as my stories will reveal. But the reasons executives fail to "scale"—that is, adapt their leadership capabilities to their growing businesses' needs—remain fuzzy. It's simply assumed that there's an entrepreneurial personality and an executive personality—and never the twain shall meet. I don't think that's true. I believe most executives can learn to scale if they're willing to take a step back and admit to themselves that their old ways no longer work.

Over the past four years, I've worked closely with more than 100 entrepreneurs and seen them struggle to adapt as their companies grow beyond a handful of employees and launch a new product or service. In the process, I've observed that the habits and skills that make entrepreneurs successful can undermine their ability to lead larger organizations. The problem, in other words, is not so much one of leadership personality as of approach. A leader who scales is able to jettison habits and skills that have outlived their usefulness and adapt to new challenges along the way.

I've identified four tendencies that work for leaders of business units or small companies but become Achilles' heels for those same individuals when they try to manage larger organizations with diverse needs, departments, priorities, and constituencies.

The first tendency is loyalty to comrades—the small band of colleagues there at the start of the enterprise. In entrepreneurial mode, you need to lead like you're in charge of a combat unit on the wrong side of enemy lines, where it's all for one and one for all. But blind loyalty can become a liability in managing a large, complex organization. The second tendency, task orientation—or focusing on the job at hand—is critical in driving toward, say, a big product launch, but excessive attention to detail can cause a large organization to lose its way. The third tendency, single-mindedness, is an important attribute in a visionary who wants to unleash a revolutionary product or service on the world. Yet this quality can harden into tunnel vision if the leader can't become more expansive as the company grows. And the fourth

Idea in Brief

It's well known that many executives who excel at starting businesses or projects fizzle out—in other words, they fail to "scale"—as their ventures grow. But the reasons have remained fuzzy. In this article, leadership coach John Hamm identifies four management tendencies that work for small-company or business-unit leaders but become Achilles' heels as those individuals try to run larger organizations. The first tendency is loyalty to comrades. In entrepreneurial mode, you need to lead as though you're in charge of a combat unit on the wrong side of enemy lines. But blind loyalty can become a liability in managing a complex organization. The second tendency, task orientation, is critical in driving toward a big product launch, but excessive attention to detail can cause a large organization to lose sight of its long-term goals. The third tendency, single-mindedness, is important in a visionary unleashing a revolutionary product or service on the world but can limit the company's potential as it grows. And the fourth tendency, working in isolation, is fine for the brilliant scientist focused on an ingenious idea. But it's disastrous for a leader whose expanding organization increasingly relies on many other people. Leaders who scale deal honestly with problems and quickly weed out nonperformers. They see past distractions and establish strategic priorities. They learn how to deal effectively with diverse employees, customers, and external constituencies. And, most important, they make the company's continuing health and welfare their top concern.

tendency, working in isolation, is fine for the brilliant scientist focused on an ingenious idea. But it's disastrous for a leader whose burgeoning organization must rely on the kindness of customers, investors, analysts, reporters, and other strangers.

Leaders who scale overcome these tendencies by dint of self-discipline, listening to and seeking input from others, and being willing to shift their outlook.

They deal honestly with problems and quickly weed out nonperformers. They see past distractions and establish strategic priorities. They make concerted, sometimes uncomfortable efforts to do what doesn't come naturally to them for the team's sake. And they learn to work with and communicate to diverse employees, customers, and external constituencies. Most important, they make the company's continuing health and welfare their top concern.

The following stories are about CEOs of technology start-ups, and they're composites of individuals with whom I've worked as an investor, board member, and coach. (The CEOs have all been given pseudonyms here.) Technology start-ups make good case studies because their lack of bureaucracy, compressed product development time, intense relationships, and vulnerability to bottom-line vicissitudes throw leadership challenges into high relief. They yield lessons that apply not only to entrepreneurs as their companies grow but also to project or department leaders as they take on bigger responsibilities in organizations of any size. As we shall see, the ability to effectively lead a project, department, or organization beyond the start-up stage depends on whether or not the executive is hampered by the four hazardous tendencies outlined here.

The Scaling Challenge

Business school courses can't really teach students to deal with people objectively, to think strategically, to create loyalty within a diverse workforce, and to impress customers and investors. These capabilities derive from experience that the new CEO may not yet have. No wonder so many entrepreneurs fail to become self-sufficient leaders as their businesses increase in complexity.

Without these skills, most new CEOs fall back on what has worked well for them before—even though these old approaches often don't fit the current problem. A product manager turned CEO may believe the next product will turn a profit. An entrepreneur who cut his teeth in marketing may respond to increasing competition with a new ad campaign. Faced with shrinking revenues, an accountant who's started a company may focus on reducing costs.

But most often, the fledgling CEOs I've observed fall into some of the traps outlined below, any one of which can be fatal to a leader's career, and even to the company being led. These entrepreneurs aren't aware that by clinging to their existing strengths and habits, they risk creating dysfunctional companies.

Let's examine the four tendencies that can prevent executives from scaling.

Loyalty to Comrades

Excessively loyal CEOs may be the best friends you could ever have, but they are the growing organization's worst enemies. That fault is understandable enough; after all, team allegiance significantly contributes to company success. But when leaders fail to see and respond to a team member's weaknesses, they place the company at risk.

Take Jason, the founder of a company specializing in wireless technology. Jason was enthusiastic and tireless in recruiting his start-up team of 20. As a loyal comrade to the cadre of smart engineers he'd befriended in graduate school and kept in touch with over the years, Jason was able to tap into his old-buddy network to build a highly competent team. Among Jason's friends was Mark, an engineering professional with whom he had never worked but felt confident would be a brilliant hire. That's because Mark had previously been a technical development manager for a large enterprise-software company. Jason courted Mark assiduously, enticing him with the opportunity to influence the start-up's strategy and make a pile of money if the venture was successful. When Mark decided to take the job, Jason was thrilled.

At first, Mark seemed like an excellent fit. He was enthusiastic about the technology, and people loved working for him. But as the company prepared to launch its first product, Mark's team wasn't equal to the engineering challenge. Accustomed to more development time and a larger staff, Mark was unable to keep up with his job's demands, and his team failed to meet a critical product milestone.

When a board member first raised the subject of Mark's performance, Jason responded with airy promises: "We're almost there with the code freeze," and "We just need another round of tests." When pressed, Jason made excuses. He insisted that Mark was working very hard, the technology was complex, and the competition was stiff. Jason refused to fire his friend even after competitors beat the company to market with a wireless product that quickly became the industry's de facto standard. Revenues took a nosedive. Then came the layoffs. Eventually, the investors shut down the company.

Such stubborn loyalty, at the expense of an organization's success, is surprisingly common. But leaders who scale, while not lacking in sympathy toward individuals, understand that the organization's success depends on every team member's strengths. These leaders understand that their first allegiance must be to a broad community of employees, customers, and investors, and to the fundamentals of the business—not to any single friend.

A good example of a leader who didn't let loyalty stand in the way of smart business is Sandy, the CEO of a small but growing organization that provides DSL broadband service. Like Jason, Sandy was a loyal friend to people she'd known since her career began. She brought in an affable, outgoing college chum, Mike, to run the start-up's technical sales department. After six months on the job, however, Sandy began to suspect that Mike needed to be more aggressive. Though he had responded to some requests for proposals, he often didn't follow up. When a promising prospect passed over Sandy's company in favor of a competitor that had an inferior product, Sandy started asking questions. First, she approached Anne, one of Mike's sales managers, about his performance. Visibly upset, Anne complained that she'd had to pick up Mike's slack; 80-hour weeks had taken their toll, and she wasn't sure how much longer she could keep up the pace. Next, Sandy checked with the CFO, who didn't deliver any better news about Mike's performance. If Mike wasn't able to clinch a deal with a very important prospect, the CFO said, the company would miss a huge revenue opportunity necessary to meet expenses.

Sandy decided that Mike had to go, but she wasn't cold about it. Empathetic and respectful, Sandy made it clear that their partnership just wasn't working. She acknowledged that Mike had left a great job to join her start-up, but now it was flirting with failure. After laying out the details of the potentially disastrous situation, she said she had no choice but to terminate Mike's employment, explaining that her decision was nothing personal and she hoped they would remain friends. When Mike left, Sandy became acting head of technical sales until she found a replacement. The company survived.

Task Orientation

Executives who focus on the job at hand—particularly those who have done well in operations, product development, or finance—are the weight lifters of the business world.

They execute brilliantly with demanding short-term assignments, but long-term strategy is often beyond them. As their companies grow, they often fail to establish strategic priorities.

Marvin, an enormously ambitious CEO of a Web services company, was that type of executive. Armed with an advanced degree in computer science, he ran product development for a firm that held a successful IPO during the dot-com era. After cashing in his stock options, Marvin pursued his dream of founding his own company.

At the outset, Marvin's task-oriented style served him well. He hired an impressive core team of engineers and set them to work on one critical task: developing a working prototype for a clearly differentiated product. Marvin's intense focus on this effort impressed venture capitalists, who rewarded him with a generous first round of financing.

As the company put out the product and expanded to 95 people, Marvin's to-do list grew. His long list of "critical" items included cutting a deal with Dell, hiring a sales VP, getting a big-name CEO on the board of directors, setting a strategy for further technology development, moving into new offices, and launching an intensive public relations and advertising campaign. Marvin delegated all these tasks to department managers, then rode herd on them. Twice a week, he required managers to update him on their projects' status. Employees made progress, but Marvin abhorred a vacuum: As soon as they completed one task, he'd fill their lists again. At first, the staff enjoyed being so busy. But within six months, people began to feel overwhelmed. Adding to their frustration was the fact that all final decisions had to pass through Marvin, who refused to make trade-offs. To him, all tasks demanded equal focus. Processes slowed. The marketing plan drifted.

No one was more dismayed or surprised than Marvin when a competitor beat his company to market with a new product and inked a significant deal with Dell. And no one was more to blame. In confusing tasks with goals, Marvin had lost control of his company's direction. The organization muddled along as a third-tier player until a competitor acquired the company at a bargain-basement price.

Leaders able to scale, by contrast, understand the importance of a streamlined strategy. They learn to extract three or four high-level goals from a longer list and focus their teams accordingly. And in the face of a new threat or opportunity, they release people from promises that were made at a different point in the development process, allowing them to delay or cancel goals they had committed to when they made sense.

Harry, the founder of a small content-management company, understood that a well-developed, simple strategy is the most important pillar of any business. He knew that his company first needed to focus on beating the competition and thus urged employees to concentrate on three activities in service to that goal: consolidating product lines, winning business away from a particularly fierce rival, and focusing on selling to companies with at least 1,000 users. This was Harry's mantra, and he repeated it at every opportunity, every day, to everyone.

That's not to say Harry's company left all other important tasks undone. Rather, Harry let employees set them aside so they could concentrate on the primary goal of beating the competition. For example, when it became clear the sales department had been focusing on customers of various sizes—many small, a few medium, and three large—Harry told the salespeople to forget about small customers.

Now, Harry understood that his strategy might be off the mark. After all, he had no crystal ball telling him that the direction he had chosen was the right one. So he availed himself of that rudder on which scalable leaders rely: the quarterly strategy audit. Every three months, Harry gathered the company's senior managers, directors, advisers, and business colleagues to review current strategy. During the four-hour meeting, the group would force itself to distill, from a list of ten, three key initiatives to be accomplished during the next 90 days. The most difficult part of the process was letting go of the remaining seven initiatives on the list. Still, the group emerged having established a simple, yet well-thought-out, plan that every employee could easily understand and follow and that could be altered the subsequent quarter, if need be. As one executive stated, "We might be wrong, but we aren't confused."

Harry was able to scale because he learned to focus on what was crucial and, in doing so, he could balance competing forces in order to set clear goals for his employees. In many ways, Harry mirrored the approaches of scalable founders-cum-leaders like Dell and Gates, who have been willing to halt extraneous activities and refocus all efforts on a few key accomplishments.

Single-Mindedness

We all admire disciplined people, and in start-ups, laserlike focus on the quality and differentiation of a new product or service is an important asset. But a

Testing for scalability

If you're thinking about turning an entrepreneur into a large-company CEO, look before you leap. A prospect can seem stunning on paper or during an interview but can disappoint in practice. The following questions can help reveal what's beneath the surface.

Question:	To determine:	To test for:
1. Have you ever fired someone? Describe what happened.	How quickly does the candidate deal with nonperformers?	loyalty
2. Pick three priorities from a sample list of ten.	Does the candidate think strategically?	task orientation
3. Describe a situation in which you were wrong and how you dealt with it.	Does the candidate learn from humbling experiences?	single-mindedness
4. What do you see as your external role in this position?	Is the candidate interested in evangelizing?	working in isolation
5. Describe your dream house.	Does the candidate have visionary capacity?	task orientation
6. What was the scariest moment in your professional career?	Is the candidate courageous?	single-mindedness
7. If you had to fire either your marketing or engineering VP, whom would you fire first?	Does the candidate protect like-minded people?	loyalty
8. What would you do if your top salesperson was distracted, and sales were falling apart as a result?	Can the candidate separate performance issues from excuses?	loyalty
9. What did you like and dislike about your last job?	Does the candidate blame others? Is he or she enriched by experience?	single-mindedness, loyalty
10. If you could return to school and study something new, what would it be?	Is the candidate a curious learner?	single-mindedness

leader's devotion to a single issue can also damage a growing organization. An insulated leader who doesn't communicate with and listen to employees with distinct opinions can end up losing their allegiance.

Sanjit, the founder of a company specializing in fiber-optic systems, was a serious technologist deeply involved with the theoretical aspects of his organization's industry niche. During the start-up stage, Sanjit's obsession was invaluable: Investors were very impressed with his understanding of and belief in the technology. His passion also appealed to the group of ten like-minded technologists he'd hired to build the company's breakthrough products. Because they shared his vision, Sanjit didn't have to spend a lot of time rallying the troops or discussing the company's strategy. His team members were convinced that when their product entered the market, it would be a runaway hit. Their enthusiasm and energy were palpable.

But as the company recruited a more diverse workforce to handle sales and run operations, Sanjit remained absorbed in the technology alone. Indeed, he had no interest in anything aside from fiber optics. He dismissed, ignored, or openly criticized marketers, salespeople, and administrators who failed to appreciate the finer points of the company's technology. And he ended up with unhappy employees, many of whom arrived not a minute before nine and left at the stroke of five each day. They gossiped about one another and picked interdepartmental quarrels. Marketers blamed technical writers for not providing data-sheet information; tech writers blamed engineers for failing to provide specifications; engineers blamed product managers for dragging their feet with outside partners. Meanwhile, the company failed to attract intelligent contributors or keep the ones it had. Like Marvin's Web services company, Sanjit's organization limped along until it was acquired for next to nothing.

Sanjit sacrificed employee loyalty to his own single-mindedness. By contrast, executives who scale learn to listen to others and take their opinions into account. They grow with their companies because they realize that their passion is not the only one that matters, and they intentionally broaden their perspective to encompass a range of endeavors.

Todd was a CEO who could see beyond his own area of interest. He was an engineer whose start-up developed and marketed software applications for wireless devices. Like Sanjit, Todd was fascinated by the technology and fervently believed that his software concept was not only groundbreaking but also potentially world changing. In response to such enthusiasm, investors wrote him substantial checks.

As the company grew, however, Todd realized that it could not live on technological excellence alone. So, unlike Sanjit, Todd paid more attention to issues that didn't revolve around the technology. He asked the public relations manager, for example, to explain how reporters thought and worked; he encouraged salespeople to describe their customer interactions. Each Friday, Todd held an all-hands meeting outlining progress toward goals and publicly acknowledging the good work of contributors, including administrative assistants and shipping clerks. And in working with his direct reports, Todd stressed the importance of making team members feel valued.

By seeking input and information from others, Todd deepened his understanding of their agendas and concerns. Because he encouraged coworkers to take pride in their contributions, they rewarded him with renewed commitment. In the end, his company scored an impressive second round of financing and secured major deals that placed it at the top of its sector.

Working in Isolation

An embryonic idea demands protection; in fact, the gestational development itself is excitingly secretive. But after the birth of the product or the idea, the internal focus must shift, lest it impede responsiveness to market demands for the finished product.

David, the founder of a software company focusing on e-mail security, was a talented programmer who enjoyed working with his engineering group on developing the first product. An introvert by nature, David liked to work in the cloistered start-up environment, where everyone was devoted to the product. David's diffidence didn't bother his few employees. Nor did he feel the need to impress anyone outside his company. Because the organization was small, and because David and his friends and family were the sole investors, he didn't need to reach out.

Then the time came to launch and market the product, and David found all kinds of ways to remain sequestered. As production deadlines loomed, he extended development cutoff dates. He tweaked packaging copy "just one more time." He canceled meetings with the public relations agency arranging press and analyst meetings. When a reporter called for a pre-arranged interview, David made sure he was in a meeting. Exasperated, his marketing director finally volunteered to deal with the press in David's place. As a result of David's refusal to meet with journalists, the new product was ranked as an also-ran in an important magazine review. Eventually, the board replaced David with someone more comfortable in the evangelist role.

Introverted entrepreneurs are often brilliant, but leaders who endure know that success requires some glad-handing and that they have to present their company to the world. Consider Simon, CEO of a small biotech company. A biochemist by training and an introvert by nature, Simon spent his professional career in large corporate research labs before being tapped to head a biotech spin-out. His ability to hunker down with his team in the lab helped get the start-up's flagship product off the ground.

A year into his tenure, Simon realized that the sales reps were targeting the wrong people in customer organizations. They were selling to midlevel managers, not directors and vice presidents. Sales sagged and the company was running out of capital as a result. Simon realized that he'd better start meeting with new investors, customers, analysts, and the media before it was too late.

Simon forced himself to become a public face for the company. He worked with a media strategist to develop an action plan. He hired a coach who taught him how to appear confident and natural in press interviews. He cold-called both customers and large investment banks. He also contacted top-level salespeople in public companies, persuading two of them to join his team. And when a large customer had to choose between his and a competitor's offerings, Simon stepped in and helped close the sale.

Flounder or Fly?

Clearly, addressing the problems of loyalty to comrades, task orientation, single-mindedness, and working in isolation during a company's formative stages will allow the founder to flourish over the long haul. On rare occasions, people rise to the scaling challenge without any special effort. More often, those who scale do so with outside help—say, the feedback of an involved board member, a coach, a mentor, or a facilitator. But entrepreneurs who grow into leaders almost always scale because they are open to learning. They want to be molded by new experiences and to improve their leadership selves. In fact, leaders who scale do so regardless of background, skill, and talent. Rather, they scale because they take deliberate steps to confront their shortcomings and become the leaders their organizations need them to be. Instead of floundering, they learn to fly.

JOHN HAMM is a partner at Redpoint Ventures in California and a former CEO of Whistle Communications, a technology firm acquired by IBM in 1999.

Originally published in December 2002. Reprint R0212J

Meeting the Challenge of Corporate Entrepreneurship

by David A. Garvin and Lynne C. Levesque

FOR LARGE COMPANIES, creating new businesses is the challenge of the day. After years of downsizing and cost cutting, corporations have realized that they can't shrink their way to success. They've also found that they can't grow rapidly by tweaking existing offerings, taking over rivals, or moving into developing countries. Because of maturing technologies and aging product portfolios, a new imperative is clear: Companies must create, develop, and sustain innovative new businesses. They must become Janus-like, looking in two directions at once, with one face focused on the old and the other seeking out the new.

Corporate entrepreneurship is, however, a risky proposition. New ventures set up by existing companies face innumerable barriers, and research shows that most of them fail. Emerging businesses seldom mesh smoothly with well-established systems, processes, and cultures. Yet success requires a blend of old and new organizational traits, a subtle mix of characteristics achieved through what we call balancing acts. Unless companies keep those opposing forces in equilibrium, emerging businesses will flounder.

In this article, we first describe the management issues facing companies that pursue new-business creation, as well as the usual problematic responses. We then explore a number of the most critical balancing acts companies must perform, the choices they entail, and the risks corporations face when they fail to get the balance right. We conclude with a look at the hybrid systems that are often needed to support these balancing acts, focusing in particular on IBM's Emerging Business Opportunity management system because of its success in mastering several of them simultaneously.

The Two-Cultures Problem

It's no secret that corporations are designed to ensure the success of their established businesses. Existing operations, after all, account for the bulk of their revenues. Finely tuned organizational systems support current customers and technologies. The operating environments are predictable, and executives' goals are stability, efficiency, and making the most of incremental growth.

New businesses are quite different, with cultures all their own. Many are born on the periphery of companies'

Idea in Brief

To trounce rivals, your company must innovate. But most new ventures set up by established businesses fail.

Why? Companies adopt one of two extreme approaches to corporate entrepreneurship—each of which has flaws. Some firms house new ventures in isolated divisions. When these firms later try to integrate fledgling enterprises with the mainstream, power struggles erupt between innovation leaders and division executives. Other companies charge *all* managers with nurturing innovative ideas. But preoccupied with their existing businesses, managers neglect new projects they consider diversions.

Authors Garvin and Levesque suggest a better approach: **balancing** elements from your new *and* old businesses.

Consider new product strategy. Creating successful innovations requires both new-business open-mindedness— "Let's try it and see how customers react"—with old-business discipline—"Let's think systematically about the market and develop a hypothesis for testing our business model." Another balancing act: mixing operational experience with inventiveness. For instance, staff new ventures with "Mature Turks"—managers who have successfully run larger businesses but also readily challenge convention.

Strike the right balance between new and old, and you sweeten the odds that innovative ventures will find a home in your company *and* score successes in the market.

established divisions; at times, they exist in the spaces in between. Their financial and operating models are seldom the same as those of existing businesses. In fact, most new business models aren't fully defined in the beginning; they become clearer as executives try new strategies, develop new applications, and pursue new customers. Because of the high levels of uncertainty associated with new ventures, they need adaptive organizational environments to succeed.

Idea in Practice

Garvin and Levesque provide these guidelines for balancing old and new.

Balance Trial and Error with Discipline

- Narrow the playing field. Encourage expansive thinking, then screen promising new ideas using criteria such as attractiveness of markets and technologies.

  Example: German manufacturing firm Henkel asked employees to identify problems they had experienced with its detergent products and to propose new business ideas that could address those problems. Employees emailed 1,000-plus proposals. An "invent team" rated ideas based on assessments of market size and Henkel's existing technical capabilities—shrinking the list to 50 promising ideas.

- Learn from small samples. Closely observe a few customers in action, to get ideas for new products and services. At Procter & Gamble, for example, managers spend time in consumers' homes, watching them cook and clean, before launching new products.

Balance Experience with Inventiveness

- Acquire new capabilities instead of developing everything from scratch. Consider time required to develop skills internally, availability of needed new skills in the open market, and ease with which outside capabilities can be integrated into your organization.

- Force new and old businesses to share responsibility for operating decisions. You'll enable the new business to leverage

The distinctive features of new businesses present three challenges. First, emerging businesses usually lack hard data. That's particularly true when they offer cutting-edge products or when their technologies aren't widely diffused in the marketplace. The difficulty, as one technology strategist told us, is that "it's established business strengths.

Example: Expo Design Center used to operate independently of parent Home Depot, though the two sold related products. Then Home Depot brought buyers from both entities together. They now work on the same floor of an office building and jointly make decisions on common purchases. This balancing has netted them large savings from the 25% of vendors that Home Depot and Expo Design share.

Balance Integration and Autonomy

- Establish criteria in advance for handoffs. New ventures protected by corporate sponsorship often prefer to stay under the corporate umbrella, where they enjoy privileged treatment and looser controls. To ease eventual integration into the existing business-unit structure, agree in advance on handoff criteria—such as revenue thresholds or number of customers.

- Employ hybrid organizational forms. Mix formal authority with informal oversight and support; for instance, through new venture councils and oversight committees.

Example: To support its shift from commodity to specialty chemicals, Ashland Chemical created its Strategic Expansion Project Board, comprised of the CEO and all group VPs. The board identified and funded high-potential projects that crossed traditional business boundaries. Once projects became operational, they moved to the Commercial Development Group, whose head reported directly to the CEO.

hard to find marketplace insights for markets that don't exist." Financial forecasts are also undependable. Large errors are common, a fact that led one printing and publishing company to call its early-stage financial numbers SWAGs, short for "scientific wild-assed guesses."

Second, new businesses require innovation, innovation requires fresh ideas, and fresh ideas require mavericks. We've heard too many stories of leaders trapped by conventional thinking: Microsoft's wariness of open-source software, Polaroid's grudging move into digital cameras, GM's and Ford's reluctance to embrace hybrid cars, media companies' distaste for blogs, and so on. Some degree of unconventional thinking is essential for new businesses to take hold, but many radical ideas are foolish or unfounded. Most mavericks, sadly, can't tell the difference between good and bad ideas. They persist in defending pet themes, demand repeated hearings, and refuse to take no for an answer. The dilemma, says Home Depot CEO Robert Nardelli, is that "there's only a fine line between entrepreneurship and insubordination."

The third challenge is the poor fit between new businesses and old systems. That's particularly true of systems for budgeting and for human resource management. Corporate budgeting systems favor established businesses because incremental dollars usually provide higher financial returns when invested in known markets rather than unknown ones. New businesses are therefore difficult to finance for long periods, and in times of austerity, they are the first to face funding cuts. In a similar spirit, companies design HR systems to develop executives whose operational skills match the needs of mature businesses—not the strategic, conceptual, and entrepreneurial skills that start-ups require. In both cases, the answer isn't to proceed haphazardly but, as we shall explain later in this article, to modify systems so they are less biased against new businesses.

Why Traditional Responses Fail

Faced with these challenges, corporations respond with one of two approaches. Some disperse the task of new-business creation, assigning it to existing divisions, while others centralize it, lodging it in special-purpose divisions or venture groups. Both approaches have delivered mixed results.

Diffused Responsibility Fizzles Out

In an organization where every executive shares responsibility for new-business creation, the CEO expects employees to be as committed to turning new ideas into new businesses as they are to expanding mature ones. Some companies impose aggressive targets to motivate managers—at 3M, the poster child for this approach, 30% of sales must come from products developed in the last four years—and they link the achievement of those targets to every employee's compensation.

The main drawback of this approach is that it's easy for traditional businesses to dominate new ones. Veteran employees often choose to ignore incentives and suppress new ideas, especially those that render existing skills obsolete or require new ways of working. RR Donnelley, the U.S. printing giant, failed in its first attempt to make digital printing popular, largely because of internal resistance. Its sales managers were accustomed to selling long-term contracts to customers' purchasing managers on the basis of personal relation-ships and the price per page. They were uncomfortable selling solutions to senior managers, which the digital business demanded, and wouldn't share expertise with the digital-printing division or send orders its way. Since they were able to make their numbers the old-fashioned way, no one could point a finger at them. As one Donnelley executive observed, resistance to the new business often took the form of the "Donnelley nod"—an apparently supportive shaking of the head but, in truth, a signal of lack of commitment.

For related reasons, a new business that doesn't fit with the company's existing product lines or markets frequently has trouble finding an organizational home. Few general managers are willing to assume responsi-bility for projects they privately view as diversions. In some cases—as with Home Depot's Floor Store, which the retailer launched in July 2000 to sell flooring and carpeting products—the fledgling business is shunted from district manager to district manager and from di-vision to division, which doesn't allow it to establish a foothold. The new venture fails to attract influential sponsors and so won't receive sufficient resources or attention to survive.

In other cases, the pressure to create new businesses becomes so dominating that it overwhelms the organi-zation. A cowboy culture results; in its wake comes a loss of financial and operating discipline. The classic example of this problem was Enron in the late 1990s, which rewarded executives for their ability to launch new trading businesses in the mold of its successful natural gas business. The result: an outpouring of trading businesses—coal, water, pulp and paper, broadband, and (later) media services, freight services, data storage, and semiconductors—that made less and less strategic and financial sense. Very few of Enron's second- and third-generation businesses became profitable, which paved the way for the company's downfall.

Centralization Isolates

Concerned by their poor track records of new-business creation, many companies decided that the wisest course was to completely separate new ventures from existing divisions. In the 1970s and 1980s, these efforts took the form of internal corporate venture divisions, special-purpose groups that companies charged with launching and nurturing the lion's share of new businesses. In the 1990s, many businesses launched corporate venture capital groups that mimicked the operation of venture capitalists by providing new businesses with arm's-length funding, disciplined oversight, and advice. Boeing, DuPont, and Exxon were among those that established corporate venture divisions, while companies like Intel, Lucent, and Xerox set up corporate venture capital groups.

Both approaches focus on nurturing new businesses in their formative stages. However, the challenges come later, when it's necessary to integrate fledgling businesses with the mainstream. Because centralized new-venture groups magnify the clash between the old and the new cultures, suspicion and fractious relationships are common, as are power struggles between new-business managers and division leaders. Over time, integration becomes more problematic, and companies must either spin off the new businesses or shut them down. The result, as Norman D. Fast wrote in *The Rise and Fall of Corporate New Venture Divisions,* is that centralized groups typically have "a long-term mission but a short-term life span." In fact, corporate venture groups in the United States last, on average, only between four and five years, according to Paul Gompers and Josh Lerner in *The Venture Capital Cycle.*

Balancing Acts

Companies should avoid either-or approaches to corporate entrepreneurship because they place the old and new cultures in conflict with each other. A new approach is called for, one that melds those cultures while avoiding extreme behavior. Lean too much in one direction, and the process drifts out of equilibrium; get the balance right, and corporate entrepreneurship will flourish. With apologies to F. Scott Fitzgerald, the test of a first-rate company may well be its ability to hold two opposing ideas at the same time and still function.

Corporations must perform balancing acts in three areas: strategy, operations, and organization.

Develop Strategy by Trial and Error
New businesses operate in highly ambiguous environments. Ambiguity isn't the same as uncertainty, as executives are realizing (see, for instance, Nitin Nohria and Thomas A. Stewart, "Risk, Uncertainty, and Doubt,"

HBR February 2006). In uncertain environments, the options are reasonably clear, and the likelihood of different outcomes can be assessed. In ambiguous environments, the full range of alternatives and outcomes isn't known, leading to many possible directions and evolutionary paths. The high levels of ambiguity in new businesses imply that corporate entrepreneurs won't get it right the first time. Because hard numbers are difficult to come by and strategic options are difficult to identify, past practices, too, offer little guidance. Experimentation is essential. Managers must begin with hypotheses about what will work and what won't; then, they should search for ways of validating or invalidating their preconceptions, knowing that first-cut strategies will change over time.

When taken to extremes, however, this approach can be counterproductive. Countless studies have shown that technologies in search of a market rarely succeed. In fact, many new businesses struggle for years because top management, hoping that one more trial will lead to success, is unwilling to close them down.

Overcoming these problems requires a balancing act that combines open-minded opportunism ("Let's try it and see how customers react; we'll make changes based on what we hear and keep at it until we get it right") with disciplined planning ("Let's think systematically about the market and the proposed technology, formulate a hypothesis about customer needs, design experiments to test our hypothesis, and repeat the process until we're sure we've got the right product, technology, and business model"). Here are five ways in which executives can couple trial and error with rigor and discipline.

Narrow the playing field. Unguided searching is an inefficient way of finding new ideas. Companies need some criteria to narrow the range of potential choices and to judge whether a technology or market presents a desirable opportunity. The goal isn't to be definitive but to scope out certain areas of promise. Smart companies identify sectors that may be worth pursuing, first by applying screens based on the attractiveness of markets and technologies, and later by combining them with executives' best judgments about promising industry trends. GE evaluates new business ideas with an eye toward increasing the scope of its operations: All new businesses must take the company into new territory— a new line of business, region or country, or customer base—and also have the potential to generate at least $100 million in incremental sales in three years' time.

The most effective companies combine brainstorming, usually at the divisional level, with corporate criteria for reducing the list of ideas. In the early 2000s, Henkel, the German consumer and commercial products company, asked employees what consumer needs they had identified when using its laundry and home care products and if those needs suggested any new business ideas. Within 48 hours, top management received more than 1,000 proposals by e-mail. It then set up a ten-person "invent team," which rated each idea on a ten-point scale based on assessments of market size, whether Henkel had the necessary technical knowledge in-house, whether the proposal fit the

Entrepreneurial Equilibrium

CORPORATIONS CAN GROW NEW businesses by performing three kinds of balancing acts.

Balance trial-and-error strategy formulation with rigor and discipline.

- Narrow the range of choices before diving deep.
- Closely observe small groups of consumers to identify their needs.
- Use prototypes to test assumptions about products, services, and business models.
- Use nonfinancial milestones to measure progress.
- Know when—and on what basis—to pull the plug on infant businesses.

Balance operational experience with invention.

- Appoint "mature turks" as leaders of emerging businesses.
- Win veterans over by asking them to serve on new businesses' oversight bodies.
- Consider acquiring select capabilities instead of developing everything from scratch.
- Force old and new businesses to share operational responsibilities.

Balance new businesses' identity with integration.

- Assign both corporate executives and managers from divisions as sponsors of new ventures.
- Stipulate criteria for handing new businesses over to existing businesses.
- Mix formal oversight with informal support by creatively combining dotted- and solid-line reporting relationships.

brand, and whether a launch was feasible within a year. Over one weekend, the team managed to shrink the list to just 50 high-potential ideas.

Learn from small samples, closely observed. In ambiguous environments, the deepest learning comes from interaction with a small number of customers, not from surveys of many potential users. The latter have great statistical power but seldom provide the formative insights that executives gain from ethnographic approaches. That's the tack that P&G has taken under CEO A.G. Lafley, who insists that managers stop worrying about focus groups and spend time in consumers' homes, watching them cook and clean, before launching new products. In 2000, the typical P&G marketer spent less than four hours a month with consumers; by 2004, that number had tripled. Intuit, which makes tax-preparation software, relies on a process it calls "Follow Me Home." The company sends employees to watch customers carry out accounting and tax-preparation tasks in their homes and offices, which helps uncover pain points that can lead to new opportunities. Starbucks periodically takes product development teams on "inspiration" trips to meet customers on their home turf. For example, in early 2006, one team visited many Starbucks outlets and other restaurants in Paris, London, and Düsseldorf, Germany, to get a better sense of local cultures, behaviors, and trends. Nokia used the same approach in China, India, and Nepal, to study how people with low incomes would use cellular telephones. Based on the research, the company's developers created an icon-based menu—consisting of pictures rather than letters and numbers—that allows semiliterate villagers to use cell phones.

Use prototypes to test business models. Without some tangible basis for discussion, most people find it difficult to evaluate new ideas. Prototypes are invaluable: They give life to emerging products and provide a basis for informed responses from potential users. They should be detailed enough for users to evaluate form, content, and desirability, and companies should couple them with forums for consumer debriefings, discussions, and reviews. Prototypes are particularly useful for testing assumptions about customer needs. UPS experimented with a grocery delivery business partly to determine whether it could tie that in with residential delivery of other goods such as consumer electronics products. Because the prototype locations showed that even loyal users ordered groceries only once every ten to 14 days—a frequency that didn't justify a larger residential delivery infrastructure—UPS quickly dropped the idea.

Track progress through nonfinancial measures. Trial-and-error strategy formulation shouldn't be entirely unguided—that would make it little more than guesswork. Concrete goals are essential, but in ambiguous environments, goals must take the form of project-based milestones, such as "We will conduct five customer trials in these two industries in the next three months." At times, companies can assess new businesses' progress by using leading indicators such as publicity or incorporation of product specifications into industry standards. The targets must be measurable:

"We will receive three positive mentions in trade journals and three favorable comments from industry analysts in the next two months."

Suspend judgment, but not indefinitely. The biggest risk when companies develop strategies through trial and error is that the process will continue for too long. Failures are common in new-business creation, and corporations need to be clear on when—and how—they will decide to pull the plug. New venture teams and top management must agree about the standards that will be applied to a project, the length of time it will be allowed to continue, and who decides whether to shut it down. There are many criteria for making the call—time elapsed, dollars spent, pace of technological progress, customer enthusiasm, confirmed orders, financial performance, competitors' success, and so on—but most critical is senior managers' willingness to make timely go or no-go decisions. Kodak's corporate entrepreneurship program failed in the 1990s largely because of senior managers' unwillingness to close several poorly performing new ventures, such as a copier services business, a floppy disks business, and a bioscience and pharmaceuticals business. That wasted resources and destroyed the program's credibility.

Operate with Something Old, Something New

Existing companies will enjoy an advantage in new-business creation only if they build on their strengths; otherwise, they will be no better off than start-ups that must begin with a clean slate. Novelty for novelty's sake is seldom a source of competitive advantage. At the same time, if new businesses make operating choices only by drawing on their parents' strengths, reusability and efficiency become the driving values, and time-tested but inappropriate people, processes, and systems will be the result. How do executives avoid these unhealthy extremes?

In most cases, the best combination of the old and the new entails a blend of experience and invention. Selling to preexisting customers, staffing with seasoned personnel, drawing on established distribution channels, and working with proven processes will improve the odds of creating profitable and sustainable operations. Differentiation, however, requires fresh thinking and innovative approaches to operations. To get the best of both worlds, companies should do the following:

Staff new ventures with "mature turks." Companies often put young, hard-charging mavericks in command of start-up ventures. Frequently, those executives are new to the company or haven't grown up in the business. Such people, runs the argument, are less constrained by companies' current ways of working. Unfortunately, they're also less likely to know which corporate resources are available or have the credibility to draw upon them. A better strategy, common at GE and 3M, is to put "mature turks"—managers who are already successful at running larger businesses but are also known for their willingness to challenge convention—in charge of new businesses. An observer described one such executive as "a 60-year-old with beads and a ponytail—a maverick but a through-and-through Xerox person with the credibility to get new businesses off the ground."

At times, top management must handpick leaders from a list of high-potential executives; at other times, it can find candidates by looking at annual personnel evaluations and identifying managers with high scores on entrepreneurship, innovativeness, and risk taking. In 1999, when L.L. Bean launched Freeport Studio, a brand of women's clothing, it selected employees for the new business from within the organization partly on the basis of how they answered one question: "How did you feel when you took a risk?"

Change veterans' thinking. Employees will seldom embrace a new business unless companies presell them the idea. Smart companies place division chiefs and group heads on the oversight committees or boards of promising start-up efforts. They expect familiarity to lead to understanding, and understanding to breed acceptance. Companies can also foster shared understanding by getting executives to envisage the future through exercises such as scenario planning. For years, Bill Gates took Microsoft's senior team on weeklong retreats, where discussion revolved around emerging technological trends and competitive threats. To reinforce the message, companies may sometimes need to alter incentives and promotion criteria, particularly when existing values are deeply rooted in organizations.

Develop some capabilities, but acquire others. Leaders of new businesses often feel that they must build every capability from the ground up. Not all skills are best developed from scratch, though; some can be purchased. The make-or-buy decision hinges on the availability of skills in the open market, the time needed for internal development, and the ease with which outside capabilities can be integrated into the organization. UPS preferred to make acquisitions when it needed specialized skills, as it did in 2000 with its purchase of Livingston, a Canadian logistics firm specializing in the unique documentation and technology systems required for the delivery of health care products, and its sister company Livingston Healthcare Services, in the United States. It also acquired companies when they had built relationships that would take UPS years to cultivate; that's why, in 2004, UPS bought Menlo, a freight forwarder that had 20-year ties with both customers and representatives of multimodal transportation services. In contrast, internal development was UPS's approach to developing mission-critical, customer-facing capabilities such as tracking and shipping systems, especially when the skills touched many parts of the business, involved legacy systems, and presented integration challenges.

Share responsibility for operating decisions. New businesses prefer complete control over their destinies. However, it's easy to lose perspective. Stanford's Robert Burgelman, in *Strategy Is Destiny,* quotes the head of one of Intel's start-up businesses as saying: "We created a very entrepreneurial culture that prided itself on being different from the rest of Intel. Some of this was justified. We have a different business model. . . .However, when we really looked at it, we found that we were being different for difference's sake."

When corporations force new and old businesses to share responsibility for critical choices, the former become more accepting of established practices and more successful at leveraging existing strengths. For many years, Expo Design Center operated independently of parent Home Depot, although the two businesses sold related products and could realize synergies in merchandising and procurement. Their buyers were brought together to improve efficiency when Robert Nardelli became CEO; they now sit on the same floor of an office building, at adjacent desks, and jointly make decisions on common purchases. That has led to large savings from the 25% of vendors that Home Depot and Expo Design share.

Integrate with Autonomy

A new business needs help from the parent company as it strives to develop an independent identity. That assistance usually takes the form of protection, sponsorship, and other types of support from the corporation's senior-most executives. Organizationally, the company gives the new business a direct reporting line to a respected leader, who becomes responsible for providing oversight, allocating resources, offering strategic guidance, and ensuring that its managers aren't hog-tied by the parent's rules. The leader treats the new business as an exception, free from the usual controls, performance standards, and review processes demanded of the company's mature businesses.

This approach works well—until it becomes necessary to hand the new business, which has outgrown the leader's ability to manage it as an exception, over to an existing business group. That's when resistance sets in and battles break out. Some conflict is predictable—there may be a knee-jerk "not nurtured here" response from existing businesses. Yet it does reflect some legitimate concerns. New businesses are rarely designed in ways that ensure a comfortable transition to the established organization, and the division managers who inherit them are not schooled in the requirements for successful handoffs. Those managers have good reason to worry that the infant businesses will fail and that top management will hold them responsible.

Too much independence leads to a related problem: a lack of organizational learning. At times, new businesses develop strategic and operational innovations that, should they succeed, are expected to be passed on to other parts of the company. That's why these businesses need considerable independence and protection in their youth. But if they are held too far apart from the mainstream or are regarded as threats to the existing order, the new ideas they embody will never take hold in the company. GM launched Saturn in 1990 to be a "different kind of car company," with innovative advertising, labor practices, operational processes, and sales strategies that were meant to serve as models for the rest of the organization. However, by 2004, GM had reannexed Saturn, tightly linking the business to its established factories, marketing programs, and labor contracts, partly because the company's other divisions had no desire to be "Saturn-ized."

For these reasons, we find, integration works best when it begins early in the life of a new business. Managers are more amenable to inheriting organizations that they have had a hand in shaping from infancy. The challenge is to get the balance right between identity and integration, and to make the shift at the proper time. Too much integration in the early days or a rushed handoff, and the new business will never differentiate itself. Too much early independence or corporate dominance, and established divisions will resist the integration of the new business. Companies can achieve the proper balance if they follow a few simple principles.

Assign corporate and operating sponsors. Corporate sponsors, who can be either line or staff executives, bring credibility and clout to new ventures, while operating sponsors, who are drawn from particular businesses, divisions, or groups, contribute organizational savvy and foster acceptance. Together, they are likely to give the right mix of freedom and discipline to new businesses, and to balance identity with integration. In 2006, Staples launched ten prototype rural stores. Each store reported simultaneously to the local district manager and to the company's vice president for strategic markets, who was responsible for the initiative. Such dual sponsorship helps overcome the problem of long and uncertain gestation periods. Few employees will sign up for a new business if they believe that resources will disappear when it becomes an independent business or if they sense that senior leaders are displaying on-again, off-again enthusiasm. With dual sponsorship, companies signal that the new business is a long-term commitment and that they have already given thought to its transition to maturity.

Establish criteria for handoffs. Unless there are preestablished standards for handoffs from corporate oversight to divisional ownership, companies will make those shifts very slowly. Most new businesses prefer to stay under the protective corporate umbrella, where they enjoy privileged treatment and special status, controls are frequently looser, and resources are easier to obtain. The criteria for handoffs can be quantitative (revenue or size thresholds, number of customers, market share targets) or qualitative (clarity of strategy, stability and experience of the leadership team, competitive superiority), but everyone in the company must know and agree to them in advance.

Employ hybrid organizational forms. Companies must also balance identity and integration by using innovative organizational structures. Such structures often consist of creative combinations of dotted-line and solid-line reporting relationships that mix formal authority with informal oversight. Councils and oversight committees are particularly useful. To support its shift from the commodity chemical business to specialty chemicals, Ashland Chemical created its Strategic Expansion Project Board, consisting of the CEO and all the group vice presidents. The board identified and funded projects that had significant commercial potential but cut across traditional business boundaries. The composition of the board ensured that representatives from multiple functions, businesses, and staff and line groups sat down together, combined perspectives, and worked out differences. Once projects became operational, they moved to the Commercial Development Group, whose head reported directly to the CEO.

How IBM Strikes a Balance

One company that has applied these principles is IBM. The starting point was September 12, 1999, when then-CEO Lou Gerstner learned that division managers had killed a promising project that focused on the explosive growth in biotechnology and life sciences computing. He fired off a scathing memo to his senior team, demanding to know why IBM kept missing the emergence of new industries. Executives quickly formed a task force to gather information by interviewing members of several struggling or unsuccessful start-ups within IBM, reviewing the academic literature on innovation and business creation, and benchmarking IBM's new-business development efforts against those of Cisco, Intel, Microsoft, and other large companies, as well as those of venture capitalists and entrepreneurs.

The team concluded that IBM's difficulties in starting new businesses could be traced to six root causes: a management system that rewarded execution and short-term results rather than strategic business building; a preoccupation with IBM's current markets and existing offerings; a business model that emphasized sustained profits and improvement in earnings per share rather than actions to drive higher price-earnings ratios; a financial, data driven approach to gathering and using market insights that was inadequate for embryonic markets; an absence of processes suitable for selecting, developing, funding, and terminating new growth businesses; and a lack of entrepreneurial skills. In essence, the team discovered that IBM, like many other companies, suffered from the two-cultures problem that we described earlier.

To overcome these obstacles, the task force recommended that IBM's senior executives devote more time and attention to developing emerging businesses; that the company identify and support promising opportunities; and that every business group and division develop its own sets of new businesses. Most important, executives recommended that IBM build a distinct Emerging Business Opportunity (EBO) management system to complement its existing systems.[1]

After several months, Gerstner remained concerned about the extent of the organization's acceptance of the task force's recommendations; the ability of IBM's existing processes to catch problems as new businesses grew; and the possibility that division managers might game the system. As one senior executive recalled, that led Gerstner to observe at one of the team meetings devoted to the topic: "Somebody around this table has to shepherd these efforts forward, someone who knows the culture well enough to kick the system. It can't be just some staff guy. It has to be someone with really big shoes." On July 24, 2000, Gerstner announced that he was promoting John Thompson, leader of the software group, to vice chairman and putting him in charge of the new-business effort. Thompson, a 34-year IBM veteran, had managed several product groups and had also led many cross-business initiatives, such as the pervasive-computing and life sciences programs. The appointment had an immediate impact. As one task force member put it: "When Gerstner made Thompson, the most respected group executive, vice chairman, the program got huge credibility. We knew then that Gerstner was serious."

Thompson moved immediately on several fronts. Initially, he told us, he saw his role as that of an evangelist, selling the company's commitment to emerging businesses "by preaching the story and occasionally making an example by putting someone in the doghouse." At the same time, he consolidated responsibility, bringing in the corporate strategy and technology groups for staff support. He insisted, as one of the conditions for taking the job, that he control a pool of funds to support EBOs, and IBM set aside $100 million for the purpose. Most important, Thompson started creating the development, oversight, and review processes that would form the core of IBM's Emerging Business Opportunity management system. In the process, Thompson and his successor, Bruce Harreld, artfully managed a series of balancing acts.

Leadership

Because many EBOs were in danger of falling between the cracks of established businesses, success hinged on their leaders' ability to navigate IBM's complex matrix organization to secure cooperation and support. The typical EBO leader had only four or five direct reports and otherwise relied on part-time assistance from other parts of the company, so each had to find ways to manage the activities of dozens or, occasionally, hundreds of IBM employees in different countries and business groups. Thompson therefore decided to choose EBO leaders for their experience and skill in working the system, as well as for their entrepreneurial, business-building, and creative talents.

Not surprisingly, many experienced managers had doubts about becoming EBO leaders. They perceived the move to be a step down; it was like, one of them said, "being asked to join a minor-league team after being a player in the major leagues." For this reason, and because the competencies they needed were difficult to find, IBM's senior-most executives handpicked the first EBO leaders. The top brass was involved in the process, Thompson pointed out, partly because "the line really didn't want to give those people up."

EBO leaders reported to the relevant business group heads, who also assumed primary responsibility for their performance reviews. However, IBM's mature turks also had a strong dotted-line relationship with Thompson and Harreld, who took over as IBM's EBO czar after Thompson retired in September 2002.

Strategy Development

Thompson charged EBO leaders with arriving at "strategic clarity"—which, at IBM, means having a deep understanding of the new business's marketplace, set of customers to be pursued, value proposition, existing and needed capabilities, and steps to be taken next. Unlike IBM's traditional planning processes, the EBOs' development process was exploratory, with frequent changes in direction. According to Thompson: "Sometimes it would take a year to a year and a half to get to a strategy we were happy with. You just kept iterating and iterating and iterating."

To resolve strategy issues, IBM encouraged EBO teams to engage with the marketplace. In the earliest days of a new business, when product designs and industry standards were still in flux, that often required selling a point of view to the outside world. Public relations and media communications were essential tasks, and EBO teams often worked directly with analysts, thought leaders, and technical columnists to gain positive coverage in the press. Eventually, however, mind share had to translate into market share. To that end, IBM expected teams to work with customers on in-market experiments, where they executed some elements of their business plans. The first step was to test the proposed product as a pilot or to persuade a few customers to allow IBM to incorporate the product or service into a new design (called a design-in). The EBO teams had to set targets that they hoped to achieve through the experiments, partly to acknowledge to themselves that failure was a distinct possibility.

As the results of the experiments came in, EBOs had to revise their strategies and business designs. Much of that work took place in monthly review meetings that included the EBO leader, the overseeing IBM business group or division head, representatives from finance and research, and the EBOs' czar (Thompson, then Harreld). At these meetings, Thompson and Harreld took care to establish ownership of the business development process: They set the agenda, asked the tough questions, and even held these meetings in their own offices. The reviews were rigorous and lasted several hours; one participant described them to us as "root canals." They were fundamentally different from IBM's traditional business reviews, which focused on financial performance versus plan targets. EBO reviews were much more developmental; they were designed to refine business plans rather than review the numbers.

Many EBO teams needed help defining their strategic intent; they found it difficult to set boundaries around what they wanted to accomplish. Assumptions about market needs and the business's ability to deliver were often wildly optimistic. Many teams had trouble identifying opportunities, sources of value, target customers, and the bases of sustainable competitive advantage. They had little experience with poorly defined marketplaces and had to learn the rudiments of strategic analysis. Because collaborative brainstorming and joint problem solving were the primary goals of these meetings, the process was contentious by design. A crisp presentation didn't matter. In fact, Harreld pointed out, most EBO leaders had to learn a new set of behaviors. "They were trained to answer every question and to have everything under control. I told them, 'Put it aside. The worse you look, the better this meeting is going to go.'"

Monitoring

Along with IBM's finance and corporate strategy staffs, Thompson and Harreld periodically evaluated each

EBO using three parameters: project-based milestones, financials, and assessments of business maturity. Together, those metrics satisfied IBM's numbers-oriented executives even as they encouraged the EBOs to innovate and grow.

The project-based milestones were the primary basis on which EBOs were evaluated. IBM used many kinds of milestones: marketplace acceptance (for instance, number of customer pilots, customer references, and design-ins), external perception (IBM's public image versus the competition's, mentions by key technology columnists, presentations at industry conferences), ecosystem development (number of software vendor partnerships and technology alliances), internal execution (significant product development checkpoints and announcements), and resource building (additions of solution and brand specialists to the staff, creation of an advisory committee, outreach to other parts of the organization). As one participant observed, IBM's executives expected milestones to indicate progress toward a goal: "They had to be more than just [any] nonfinancial measures that were easy to count."

The EBOs were not, however, completely free from financial scrutiny. Once a new business was up and running, IBM's finance group calculated its revenues and direct expenses. The reports provided the basis for monthly reviews that the finance group conducted with each EBO's executives. Meetings were often brief, but they served a dual purpose. They prepared emerging businesses for the financial reviews that would be required of them as they matured. In addition, they provided a check: If the expenses of an EBO were below budget but it wasn't meeting its milestones, that often meant that the IBM division funding the new venture was cutting back on investments. "That's a foul," an IBM corporate finance executive told us. "And you can only find it by looking at expenses and milestones in the same meeting."

Finally, to track how well all the EBOs were progressing, IBM's corporate strategy department developed a color-coded scoring system. It rated each EBO in three areas: developing a clear strategy, defining an executable model, and winning in the marketplace. Red identified concerns or problems, yellow signaled limited progress and unresolved issues, and green indicated sustained success. The strategy team summarized the results of these assessments in monthly and quarterly reports to senior management. These ratings also helped executives determine when the new businesses were ready to be transferred out of the EBO management system.

The true measure of any system is its results. Of the 25 business bets that IBM has made in the past five years, three have failed, and the remainder are a mix of evolving and successful businesses. In 2002, these businesses contributed more than $6 billion in additional revenues; in 2003, more than $10 billion; and in 2004, $15 billion.

Most of the new businesses are now in the hands of IBM's business groups. That transition occurred quite suddenly. Gerstner's successor, Sam Palmisano, triggered the shift when he suggested to Harreld in August

2003 that "maybe we're hugging the EBOs too closely."
Harreld responded by deciding, almost overnight, to
move 14 EBOs out of the corporate system and into
IBM's business groups. In each case, he based his decision on two simple tests of sustainability: Did the business have clear leadership? And did it have a clear
strategy? Any operational issues, he felt, were better addressed by the business group leaders than by the corporate strategy department.

The handoffs were accompanied by tightened monitoring and reporting. IBM made the business groups'
quarterly reviews more rigorous, with corporate strategy executives attending to monitor the progress of the
EBOs. Each group's monthly letter to the chairman had
to describe the status of its EBOs. In addition, Harreld
met twice a year with every business group head to review the EBOs' progress and to ensure that IBM's traditional culture wasn't choking their performance.

For companies that wish to succeed with corporate entrepreneurship, the lesson is simple: Success is not an
either-or proposition. New businesses should be nurtured through a series of balancing acts that combine
entrepreneurship and disciplined management, short-
and long-term thinking, and established and new
processes. As IBM's EBO management system shows,
when companies must choose between black and
white, the best response is often gray.

Note

1. For more details, see David A. Garvin and Lynne C. Levesque, "Emerging Business Opportunities at IBM" (A, B, and C), Harvard Business School case nos. 9-304-075, 9-304-076, and 9-304-077.

DAVID A. GARVIN is the C. Roland Christensen Professor of Business Administration at Harvard Business School. **LYNNE C. LEVESQUE** is a Boston-based consultant and researcher.

Originally published in October 2006. Reprint R0610G

Index

You don't want to miss these...

We've combed through hundreds of *Harvard Business Review* articles on key management topics and selected *the* most important ones to help you maximize your own and your organization's performance.